SUNSHINE *on* *My* SHOULDER

A Loving—Unforeseen Spiritual Journey

SUNSHINE *on* *My* SHOULDER

A Loving—Unforeseen Spiritual Journey

PATRICIA STAGG

Printed in the United States of America

Packaged by Pleasant Word, a division of WinePress Publishing, PO Box 428, Enumclaw, WA 98022. The views expressed or implied in this work do not necessarily reflect those of Pleasant Word, a division of WinePress Publishing. Ultimate design, content, and editorial accuracy of this work are the responsibilities of the author.

ISBN 1-57921-665-X
Library of Congress Catalog Card Number: 2003104801

This book is dedicated to twelve wonderful blessings that fill my life with love and inspiration—my husband, my children, and my grandchildren.

Contents

Preface

> For You created my inmost being; You knit me together in my mother's womb. I praise You because I am fearfully and wonderfully made; Your works are wonderful, I know that full well. My frame was not hidden from You when I was made in the secret place. When I was woven together in the depths of the earth, Your eyes saw my unformed body. All the days ordained for me were written in Your book before one of them came to be. (Ps. 139:13–16)

This profile of love, courage, and determination is for all who look at life and know that it comes from God, and for those who aren't sure there is a God. It's for parents and grandparents, youth and children, and everyone in between.

Our family was singled out and allowed to receive a precious gift awarded to few. What we discovered is that the world with all its illusive trappings cannot give what we received. God spoke to us in a very direct way. It had to become tangible, something we could see and touch. We had to see Him, in and through Tim. Then, through our own personal experiences, we could confidently use what was given to us to convey God's message ". . . for eyes to be opened to see and for ears to be opened to hear" (Acts 28:27).

Sunshine on My Shoulder is about Tim, a special child who grew into a special young man. Within a lifetime of afflictions and hardships, he developed a sincere compassion for the needy and the sick. God does not make mistakes and say, "Oops." And Tim did not live his life in vain. It was through his life that God was glorified.

Tim went from this world into the Lord's heavenly presence on July 9, 1998, but he left a legacy far beyond anything we could have imagined. He was blessed with gifts that made up for his physical and mental disabilities, which allowed him to make a difference in our lives and in the lives of those who knew him.

> JERRY LEWIS: Tim Stagg touched my life briefly but indelibly. In the short time I knew him, I remember that his positive spirit was invigorating and inspiring. I feel honored and grateful to have known him.
>
> I also feel the injustice of a special young man's life coming to an end due to the progression of Charcot-Marie-Tooth disease. Tragically, it's too late to save Tim's life. But it's not too late to try to save other precious lives by intensifying our commitment to help MDA-funded scientists find ways to halt the destructive effects of CMT and related neuromuscular disorders.

> I'll cherish my memory of a unique young man named Tim Stagg. He was truly an outstanding and unforgettable person. I've no doubt that those reading this account of his life will be as touched and inspired by him as I was.

I want to thank Bridget Carey from the MDA office in Chicago for all her help down through the years, and also the many others we did not see who worked behind the scenes.

When I was ready to have this manuscript proofed and edited, I prayed, "Lord, what do I do next: Who can I give it to so it will be done right?" That same morning Jane Nelson came into my office at church to see me. She had recently lost her mother and was inquiring about my mom, now ninety-two and failing.

Jane said she had more time on her hands now with her mother gone, and also because she wasn't working anymore. I asked her what kind of work she did. Her reply: "I was an editor for Moody Bible Institute publications." For a moment I was speechless! What an amazing and wonderful God. I thank Him, and I thank Jane.

I also thank Shannon Kurtz for helping proof my first draft and Carol Garrett, coworker, for additional help. These priceless friends have been a blessing to me through the final months of my putting it all together.

Introduction

My Tim, from Dad:

When I think of my Tim, I think of courage and determination like I've never known. I think of the wonderful years of joy and laughter he gave us, and his gentleness and compassion for others. I think of his very own, very special brand of common sense to overcome any obstacle. Tim was a paradox; he was retarded and yet in his own way he had an intelligence that I feel was unmatched. I won't even try to explain that except to say that those of us who were blessed with his presence will understand and need no further explanation.

I remember when Bill Cosby lost his son. Mr. Cosby said his son was his hero. I understood him because my Tim was *always* my hero. Many years ago and many times since, Tim would ask, "Dad, do you think if I was okay I would have been a good baseball or football player? Do you think I would have been good at sports?" The first time and every time from then on I would reply, "Tim, you would have been the best at anything you tried."

Many sports celebrities are heroes to many people, but I made it clear to Tim I felt so lucky because he was my true hero and also my son. Tim would look at me with that kind of shy and yet sly smile and he would say, "Really!" With that he would melt my heart. I love my Tim more than life itself and told him that every day of his life. I am not ashamed to say I still tell him that every day.

I didn't tell Tim he was my hero just to make him feel good, I sincerely meant it. Tim was physically and mentally handicapped. His physical stature was quite small, but I can say with all honesty that he was the biggest man I have ever known. I have said this before and will say it again: if I could be just half the man Tim was, it could be said, I am one heck of a man. I hope some day to measure up.

In my heart I know that God chose us to have Tim. Maybe He sent Tim to us, not so much because we were special at the time, but He sent Tim to *make* us special. And I believe Tim did just that. I don't mean to have that sound like I'm putting us on a pedestal, I don't mean it that way. When I look around at so many other families with the serious problems they have, I see an apparent lack of love and respect they display for one another. Then I look at my family and how much we all love and respect each other. It's easy for me to say that we have been blessed with something very special. That blessing came from Jesus through our Tim. I know that as sure as I am writing this.

That blessing didn't come easy. Tim caused the greatest highs and the lowest lows of my life. To have him in my presence was joy in the purest sense. At the same time, just to see him struggle to walk was a knife in my heart. Through the years, Patti and I have been through so much pain for our Tim, but nothing could have prepared us for what he endured during the last six months of his life.

I lost my older brother Tom, many years ago. I watched my dad sometimes abuse my mother until I was big enough to put a stop to it and then watched him drink himself to death. Then my mother died too. Those times of pain and grief were not easy—they wouldn't be easy for anyone. I thought, because of those losses, and all we had been through with Tim, that maybe we were prepared for his passing.

Tim died peacefully in his own bedroom. We were all there with him, and it was a very special experience for all of us. But like Tim, it too was a paradox. Because, while it was something very special for us, I know for me it began a pain and grief like I didn't believe could exist. I never thought it possible to hurt the way I do today. It is indescribable. I know with God's help and with time I will learn to live with it, but I also know I will never get over losing my Tim.

If it weren't for our Kathleen and Quinn, and Mark, Kelly and our wonderful granddaughters Amanda, Brittany, Natalie, and Bryana, and our two additions, grandson Patrick and granddaughter Brandi, all this would have been unendurable. We love our family so very much.

Tim used to call me on the intercom between the house and my office in the garage. He would say, "Hey Dad, how about going out for lunch? I'll buy." I would say, "Good idea Tim, bring your money if you're going to buy." And he would say, "I have it in my pocket." He would come out and I'd put him in the truck and off we'd go.

Burger King was his favorite place for lunch. We would get there and I would say, "Well, seeing as how you're buying I need your money." And he would say, "I got you covered, Dad," and dig in his pocket. He'd pull out a dollar and say, "That should do it." Those were very special times for me and I will never forget them. That was just one of the many, many special times we had together. As a matter of fact, any time with Tim was a special time.

I will always grieve for my Tim, but there were so many wonderful and really enchanting times with him that my memories in time will outweigh my grief. I thank the Lord for giving us our Tim for thirty-eight of the best years of our lives.

CHAPTER 1

The Meaning of Sunshine

It was June, Father's Day, and raining—but a little rain never hurt any camper. Camp gear, food, clothing and games were packed into our pop-up tent camper for an early start in the morning. My husband, Pat, having just finished a large building project, looked forward to getting away.

At the crack of dawn we headed north on our three-hour drive into Wisconsin to an area overlooking the Wisconsin River. Blackhawk Ridge was a rugged, beautiful site located in the territorial land of the legendary Indian Chief Blackhawk. It was ideal for the wilderness camping we loved.

With our three children, Kathleen, Tim, and Quinn, and one dog, Christopher, we arrived at our destination, and the skies opened to a downpour. Undaunted, we piled into the jeep that would take us and our camper to a faraway, secluded campsite. Surely the rain would stop; it had already rained a full week.

We looked forward to this getaway. It was our first campout with fifteen-year-old Tim since his seven-month hospital stay for spinal surgery the previous year. In anticipation, his excitement mounted. Being crippled, he looked forward to anything that would take him away from his normal daily routine.

Our thoughts were in unison. We all knew the sun would peek through those dark clouds at any moment. Tim sat in the front seat of the jeep wearing a poncho while the rest of us held on for dear life in the back. Quinn, who was twelve, had a grip on me as I bounced precariously on the back ledge. At the same time he held a green striped shower curtain over us as protection from Mother Nature. Pat wasn't as fortunate. Already drenched, his dark hair had become bouncy ringlets. Kathleen, now seventeen, did her best to hang on and keep from drowning.

The young man driving the jeep must have thought we were out of our minds. It was raining so hard water ran out the sleeve of his jacket when he put his arm down. I wondered if he was silently "cussin' in God's veins," the expression Tim used for anyone who would swear or misuse God's name in vain. But the driver gave no outward indication he was upset and went right along with our craziness.

Our situation grew more comical by the minute as we blessed ourselves (whatever that means) and laughed till our sides ached. A day or two of rain can be tranquilizing when you're cozy and warm, a time for telling stories and playing games. But this was ridiculous. Slap-happy, we finally reached the campsite with full certainty Mr. Sun would soon be shining.

Tim loved to talk and always chimed in with funny stories and his own unique knock-knock jokes. They were so bad you had to laugh. Being a lover of music he also knew a trillion songs and sang each one in perfect tune. That year his favorite was "Sunshine on My Shoulder Makes Me Happy" by John Denver.

When all was settled and everyone in dry clothes, a roaring fire was built. Though the rain was steady, tree branches overhead were so thick they protected us as we sat staring at the burning embers.

Christopher was exhausted. He was a mix of terrier and beagle, with long hair and a darling face like Benji, the character Disney made famous. If he could talk he would have told us he'd had about enough. And all the time he thought he was missing something when we went camping without him.

We snuggled into sleeping bags with thoughts of tomorrow being filled with sunshine on our shoulders. It was a sure thing, right? Wrong. It never stopped raining.

Tim wasn't the least bit bothered by this for he always had a positive attitude toward everything. He only saw sunshine through the rain and talked as though it was already on the horizon. All of us would turn to look outside because he was so convincing. It isn't too far-fetched for me to say that we're quite certain he did indeed see something we didn't.

After three days of water, mud, and the constant pelting on top of our camper, we needed to get away from that place. Everything now damp and soggy was again packed up. As we stood in the rain waiting for the jeep to rescue us, I held a garbage can lid over Tim's head to keep him dry. I recall how the song "Sunshine on My Shoulder" kept going around in my head.

As my thoughts tossed the song around, there was no doubt in my mind, "Tim surely was our sunshine." He never let life's rainfall take the shine out of our lives, and the impact upon us, and so many others, was exactly that same dimension: bright and illuminating.

Traveling across America

While Tim was still in the hospital recovering, Kathleen had her sixteenth birthday. Her only request, "Can we go camping?" This was a surprise to her dad and me, and we were happy to respond with a couple of days at Blackhawk Ridge. It was an opportunity to do things with her and Quinn we normally weren't able to do when Tim was with us.

Camping was affordable and made family vacations possible. Our travels took us to all parts of the country from the Catskill Mountains of New York to the Smokies in Tennessee and President Kennedy's grave in Washington with eternal flame and military guards. We toured historical paths of Mark Twain in Hannibal, Missouri, and visited Stone Mountain, Georgia, with its civil war battleground and documentation on the fall of Atlanta.

My sister Sharon, husband Ben, and their boys, Bennett and Scott Brown, lived in Georgia at that time, and we fell in love with the South. They took us to Underground Atlanta, where we enjoyed a rare experience being drawn into its attractions and lure of yesteryear. While in Roswell, Georgia, we bought a cane for Tim at an antique store. Years later, Tim met Matt Brown, the 1977 Muscular Dystrophy Poster Child, who happened to be from Roswell.

We went to Mammoth Cave in Kentucky and even found a spot to say goodnight on the grounds of Ft. Knox. The kids saluted military guards and they saluted back as army tanks rumbled down the street. The NASA Space and Rocket Center in Huntsville, Alabama, allowed us to touch Apollo 16, one of the spacecraft that went to the moon and back.

When we visited Kelly and Carmen Yates and their boys David and Greg in Elizabethton, Tennessee, they let us camp in their backyard and would you believe it actually snowed? This of course was blamed on us northerners. Here we enjoyed an honest-to-goodness southern breakfast of country ham, eggs, grits, and biscuits and gravy.

Pat smoked an occasional cigarette back then. He reminded Kelly about their army days and the comeback he gave when Pat tried to bum a smoke from him. Kelly would jokingly tell him, "I wouldn't give you R if I had you in a jug!" With his southern drawl (they talk funny) the word "air" comes out "R." And forever after, "I wouldn't give you R if I had you in a jug" was echoed with sweet nostalgia. Tim never got tired of repeating it and would use it on his dad at very appropriate times—marked with his hearty belly laugh.

The Yateses also took us for a picnic on top of Roan Mountain, the highest point in Tennessee, where four states can be seen at one time. And then they drove us to North Carolina to see the amazing Brown Mountain lights—lights that cannot be explained. While in Tennessee, we also took the kids to the American Museum of Atomic Energy in Oak Ridge.

One February day we visited my brother, Ken Minahan, in Phoenix, Arizona. We went from snow up to our knees in Flagstaff, to the dry warmth of the desert that was in full bloom because of all the snow that year.

As we left Salt Lake City and headed east toward Illinois and home, we found ourselves in the middle of a winter carnival in Steamboat Springs, Colorado. Deep snow covered downtown Main Street, so various snow races could be held in the middle of town. As long as the ground was level Tim could walk, but the deep snow was an obstacle for him and we had to carry him from one side of the street to the other. At night we watched a breathtaking candlelight procession of skiers come down the mountain directly in front of the hotel where we were staying.

These are some of the places we vacationed with the kids, who turned out to be good travelers. When we camped without Tim that summer, the four us went on a horseback, trail-ride breakfast. As we wound our way up the bluffs overlooking the Wisconsin River, the guide brought us to a place where our breakfast was prepared and waiting for us. Plans to canoe the river were made for the following day. It was sunny and hot as our paddles and the current moved us along the scenic waterway with its sandbars and ragged bluffs on either side.

We're grateful for the family memories our vacation trips gave us. Growing up with a handicapped sibling limits full family participation in most physical activities. We could camp and visit a variety of interesting and educational places, but we couldn't all canoe, hike, or go horseback riding together. But God blessed us far more abundantly!

A New Little Person

As my life evolved, it was quite remarkable how a Catholic nun's prophetic commentary would forecast what the future held for me and my family.

Tim's birth was normal. While in the hospital awaiting his arrival, I had a wonderful conversation with a lovely woman, the nun who assisted me. I don't know what prompted her to say what she did. But her profound words have been on my heart all these years, and I have had many opportunities to share them with others.

She related how everyone suffers during his or her lifetime. A minor crisis for one individual could become an all-consuming and devastating crisis for another. She went on to say how there are differences in the way people react to circumstances in their lives. A death brings on a certain level of deep grief and pain to those in mourning, but someone who might experience a much lesser trauma can feel this same level of pain.

The conclusion, I suppose, would probably depend on how people are wired to handle adversity and hardships. Now, as I think back and remember from where it was I have come, I know that a relationship with Jesus Christ makes the difference in the lives of those with hardships and suffering. And we all have hardships and suffering!

It was January 30, 1960, when Timothy Patrick, a beautiful, healthy baby joined his sister Kathleen, who was eighteen months old. Our family was complete. A hospital stay for new mothers at that time was four or five days, so I vividly recall this particular day when Pat came back from visiting the nursery.

With a bit of apprehension he said, “There’s a baby in that nursery with a real strange cry, and I hope it isn’t ours.” Later we discovered it was indeed Tim, but we didn’t know then the significance of his different cry. No medical personnel picked up on it. In-depth testing of newborns at that time was not necessarily done. Or if it was, it was not done on Tim. Our healthy baby wasn’t really as healthy as we thought.

Everything seemed normal as we settled into our new-baby-routine mode. Then, as quickly as you blink an eye, our lives were forever changed. Tim was two weeks old when his crying began. I stood and rocked him as I tried to visit with neighbors who came to welcome our new son. They left and the crying continued.

When Tim reached his third month he began sleeping all night, but the daily crying went on to some degree for nearly two years. The usual doctor checkups were kept, and after an examination for the crying we were told he was probably spoiled.

Tim was robust and the picture of health, which didn't change the fact we were constantly taking him to the doctor. His immune system wasn't fighting off colds and infections. As we coped each day, his crying just became part of our lives. Buggy and car rides normally put babies to sleep, but they only made Tim cry that much more. Nothing soothed him. There were times when he'd be sitting quietly on the floor playing, and my walking across the room was the trigger that started it again.

I was a mom, and I was tired. Exhausted was more like it. When Tim took a nap I'd lay down for mine. As I'd drift off he'd begin to cry, and many times I could not get up off that couch. It was as though I'd turned to stone, unable to move.

Kathleen, as young as she was, recalls how she and I would be playing or making cookies, doing something together, and Tim would begin to cry. Whatever we were involved in would stop. Without knowing it, the lives of Kathleen and Quinn were part of the growing experience of having a sibling who, by God's design, needed extra care. Until we understood the enormity of what we were dealing with, Tim had the care expected for normal babies. He didn't receive the extra care we now know he needed. Would we have known what he needed?

If I could change anything, it would be to have Tim all over again, especially as a baby. I would want the necessary discernment and maturity to do some things differently.

But isn't that like all of us? Who of us wouldn't change something if we could? It's always easy to have hindsight. If we were to recognize and know everything we would be the experts we all hear about. The mysterious ones with advice, those who we refer to as, "They said." And if there is one thing I know for sure, there are no experts when it comes to raising children.

What's Life All About?

There was nothing special about us. We were the neighbors next door and the people down the street—no different than other young families raising children. As time passed, however, our perspective on life changed as we learned to live with a child who really was different.

We faithfully attended church, and Tim was baptized when he was a month old. At a very young age I had been programmed to pray repetitious prayers that were passed down from family and church. But as years came and went this ritual did not lead to the fulfillment of knowing God. I grew up with a good amount of religion, its legalisms and traditions, and was never told about a relationship of far greater importance.

God seemed so remote to me. Even though I knew about God through my upbringing, my heart did not connect. Even though I knew Jesus died on the cross for the sins of the world, for my sins, I did not connect. Now thirty years old I questioned, "Was there really a God?" Because the Bible was not part of my personal life, I was not familiar with the consoling, inspirational verses of Scripture—messages of wisdom and comfort that could soothe an aching heart in time of need.

With my spirit weary and my mind clouded by doubts, I decided to stop praying altogether. I felt it was a waste of time and energy. And I needed energy. There was no way I could know that my life was slowly drifting along to a planned time and place when it would be changed forever.

CHAPTER 2

Suspicions and Surprises

Tim was about to answer the door in his underwear and he was told it wasn't nice. His reply about the neighbor who was at the door, "He's a people like we are, isn't he?"

After an early-morning errand, I returned home somewhat shaky and reached for the phone. I wanted to tell someone about how dizzy I became while driving the car. I called a friend who lived down our street and told her what had happened. Her resounding words still echo in my ears as she came back with, "Oh Pat, you're just feeling sorry for yourself." And for one long moment I couldn't believe I heard her right. But yes, that is what she said: ". . . feeling sorry for yourself."

When I recovered from her response, I was terribly convicted of my complaining spirit and vowed never to complain again. This decision was not a good one because neither family nor friends realized the scope of what it was like dealing with our young son and all the unknowns affecting him.

I was never able to cry—but now as the doctor questioned me to find the reason for the dizziness, I was sobbing and didn't know why. The only thing I could think of, and it was a second thought as I searched for an answer, was that my baby cried all the time. Stress from his crying was the cause, and I was shocked when the doctor told me I was very close to having a breakdown.

Both Pat and I had a nagging feeling that something was not right with Tim but couldn't put our fingers on what it was. Then when he was a year old my friend Cindy Denny asked me if we realized his lower legs were underdeveloped. She brought something to our attention that we did not see, but now it was obvious the calves of Tim's legs were thin and lacking muscle. As young parents we were in for a jolt.

Dr. Benjamin Rappaport was a well-known pediatrician, and going to him was a new experience. He examined Tim much more thoroughly, and with it came an amazing discovery. Tim was born without reflexes anywhere in his body. In his forty-two years of practice, Dr. Rappaport said he never saw a child without reflexes. Tim was also anemic, tongue-tied, and in need of special vitamins. All this new information was hard to believe because our family doctor had seen him many times, and none of these observations were detected. After four months of vitamins the anemia was corrected, but the nonreflex condition remained.

At twenty months, a battery of tests revealed Tim had a birth defect of the lower spine that would prevent him from running and going up and down stairs. He had a small white spot on his lower back that looked like a scar, and we wondered if it marked where the defect began. Along with this diagnosis the doctors felt he would catch up mentally to be close to normal.

Dr. Bigler, director of Children's Memorial Hospital in Chicago, told me to take Tim home and treat him as normally as possible. In all my years of caring for our special son, this turned out to be the best advice we ever received. For Tim's overall development and limitations, this attitude proved to be the biggest factor for his living a well-adjusted, quality life.

But another blow was on the way as Dr. Rappaport read me the report Dr. Bigler sent to him. In it he had written that there was a poor relationship between mother and child. As I heard those words I felt as though someone had pierced my heart. Something was evident that we did not see. I am grateful to Dr. Rappaport, who, full of compassion, showed me that report.

Years later I read an article about mothers of crying babies who become desperate and need time to recoup. They need to be away from the constant crying, but in my case, I was never away from it. Research showed how mothers would take care of their babies and all their needs, but at the same time, unconsciously withdraw. They simply needed help.

Postpartum depression is also a common condition with new mothers and recognized with some of the above symptoms. Whether that was a problem with me and my fatigue and what I now realize could have been depression, I do not know. There's evidence that postpartum depression, caused by hormonal changes and stress of a new baby, can occur up to two years after the birth.

I felt a little better when I realized there really couldn't be a good bonding relationship with a habitually crying infant. It's also common to find that some parents do not pick up on or recognize they are dealing with an abnormal situation. From this unbelievable experience, and Dr. Bigler's observation, our driving aim for Tim was to make up for lost time.

Doctors have said that even if they had known something was wrong in infancy, they never would have been able to make a correct diagnosis. Today, however, technology is so advanced that neurological problems are discovered quickly and dealt with when possible. Our special education programs make early childhood classes available for children with disabilities. They begin in infancy giving them a head start to advance their development both mentally and physically.

Tim, when still a toddler, cried during what would be normal activity for children, and several of our photos show this. After a beautiful snowfall, Kathleen, Tim, and I bundled up and went outside to build a snowman. Our picture shows the finished snowman and in the background we see Tim crying.

When we were at Deer Haven, a small hometown park with a petting zoo, Tim cried most of the day. We didn't know then that any kind of movement probably caused him pain and distress. As he went around a track in a kiddy car and later as he sat next to Kathleen on a little train that traveled around the park, he cried. And trips to visit friends were full of tension; by the time we got there I felt like I'd been run over by a truck.

Those Early Years

Tim was almost two and still not walking. Pat strung rope across the yard so he could hold on as we encouraged him to take steps on his own.

Perhaps his love for music started when Kathleen would take him by the hands and walk him to the middle of the room. Keeping in time to a melody, she'd try to get him to move his legs. One day her efforts paid off. As we watched her tugging Tim, now twenty-five months old, to the middle of the floor, he took his first successful steps alone. Kathleen was three-and-a-half and Tim was as tall as she was and heavier. Always the little mother, she patiently helped Tim develop the balance he needed.

Tim's nature can be described with one word: determination. From the day he was born his life was a struggle, but God blessed him with a mind that was far superior than we could have known or understood. This determination allowed him to achieve a lifelong series of exceptional accomplishments.

Now, though, Tim was four and still not talking. And yes, I was praying. Then one day we heard him say, "Dad." To say we were excited would be an understatement, but the unexpected happened. Tim went from not talking at all to talking nonstop. With this additional drain on our already beat-up nervous systems, we were beginning to feel the effects.

During the kindergarten year, out of the blue, Tim told me he wanted to go outside by himself. This was the first time he left my side to do something on his own, and outside he went. And yes, there were tears of relief and thankfulness for another small step of advancement. All those small steps were really big ones. For a family of a disabled child these were great big moments of triumph.

Weeks ran into months and months into years. Pat and I were on an unending roller coaster—lifted up here, shot down there. Even though Tim was walking well, other improvements we waited for were slow in coming.

His early years were difficult, and one particular time when he was six years old stands out in my mind. We wanted him to turn off a light and coached him as he stood directly in front of the switch. We repeated over and over for him to take his hand and turn the light off. He could not understand what we were asking him to do, and it became real traumatic for him. We liken it to a short circuit where his brain was not able to make the connection. As Tim grew, these kinds of situations became fewer and fewer.

Each Child So Different

Kathleen was born with olive skin, dark brown hair, and brown eyes. Tim was a towhead with white curly hair, fair skin, and brown eyes. Pat's family, the Staggs and Darrows, were known for their almond-shaped eyes and curly locks. Quinn, who was born when Tim was three, also had olive skin but looked more like me with blond hair and blue eyes inherited from the Boyle and Prokop families. He made up for everything Tim could not do, and he became the much-needed positive challenger. The Lord blessed Tim with this younger, very quiet, fast-moving, bolt-of-lightning brother. Quinn was full of electric energy. At the same time he, like Kathleen, had a gentle, kind, and caring spirit.

Tim was now playing outdoors, interacting with other kids, keeping up at his own pace. So it wasn't surprising when he and Quinn could not be found one warm summer night. Panic set in as we combed the neighborhood. In desperation, Pat went one city block over to the next street, walking and calling their names. Tim was six and Quinn was three.

Pat spotted a slightly ajar overhead garage door and without hesitation lifted it up. There they were. Quinn was perched on the seat of a large riding lawn mower. And Tim? He was standing in the corner taking hands full of ashes from a barbecue kettle and throwing them all over the garage. Screeches of laughter went up as they watched the falling ashes create great puffs of smoke.

Surely it was Quinn's idea. What are ashes for anyway? What little boy wouldn't figure they should be used for something—so why not? With their lively adventure ended, two sets of wide-eyed aliens covered with soot from head to toe were delivered safely back to our yard. Standing as if frozen, they looked up at me with wide, sad eyes. In fact, all I could see were eyes. It's a precious picture etched in my mind forever, with a little sunshine on my shoulder mixed in.

The owners of the garage insisted they wanted to clean it themselves, and I wonder to myself if they weren't sweeping and scrubbing—and cussin' in God's veins.

In the spring of 1967 we bought a home in Lake Villa, Illinois, and were ready to move from the house we rented for the past three years. Preparations with cleaning and packing were running smoothly; we wanted everything to be exactly as it was when we moved in. But how quickly that was about to change.

Directly in line with a large picture window was a beautiful burgundy-colored bush that was cherished by the owners. As I looked outside for the boys, the sight that hit my eyes made me sick to my stomach. Half of the branches of this perfectly shaped bush were broken off and lying all over the ground.

Within minutes I stood in disbelief with Quinn and Tim before the ugly remains. The expressions on their faces were as unbelieving as mine. They could see how upset I was, and their faces were beginning to look as crumpled up as mine was. I questioned them, and they denied knowing anything about it. It took several minutes as I looked, and they looked, and then . . . reality set in. Without a doubt they were the culprits, and both were guilty.

> KATHLEEN: One of my most vivid memories of my brother Tim is when we moved into our new home. Because everything was so new and different, we slept together in an upstairs bedroom. To keep each other warm at night we would sleep with our backs touching. Before I would be fully awake every morning, I would feel my eyes being pried open. Tim would be looking straight in my face and laughing at how funny I looked. It was a rude awakening but a fun start to my day. I have many memories of my brother. Some good, some frustrating, and some sad.

Reality without Wisdom

A twenty-minute drive from home brought me to Bush School, a small, low building wrapped in red brick. With only four classrooms it was easy to find my way to the one I was looking for, and I opened the door.

Chaos engulfed the room. Kids of all sizes were everywhere, and the noise was ear-splitting. Along with their pushing and shoving one another was the unbelievable sight of a boy walking on a large inside window ledge. As I looked in disbelief, there in the midst of it all was seven-year-old Tim.

A petite, sweet-looking woman in her late forties welcomed me. She was quick to explain how this was a normal school day and I shouldn't be upset by what I saw. The motion of her knitting needles never stopped as she steadily tugged at colored yarn. Meanwhile, the bedlam all around us kept up its frenzied pace.

Through the blur of a conversation I sensed a change in her tone of voice. She went from explaining why these children were acting as they were to, "There is a serious problem with your son Tim. He's much too disciplined and well behaved. He acts like a little tin soldier, and this is not at all what's expected of mentally retarded children!"

My stomach was turning and my head was swimming as I made an appointment for her to meet with us in our home. Pat and I were confused and disappointed. Is this what we, and especially Tim, had to look forward to? Was he going to survive this kind of environment day in and day out?

Tim attended regular kindergarten at Fox Lake Grade School the year before under the direction of Betsy Houghton. She made exceptions for his peculiar and erratic behavior. Her note at year's end read, "Timmy has fit in our class amazingly well. He is well liked and he enjoys the children. I shall be eager to hear of his progress." Betsy was firm, but loving, treating him with patience and understanding.

As the kindergarten year wound down, Tim was given three IQ tests by three different sources to see where best to place him. He scored 60 on all three, putting him on a lifetime intelligence level of a six-year-old.

IQ scores in the 70s are considered borderline between average and mentally retarded. And an IQ of 60 meant he was far below average. The borderline between trainable and educable was 60, and the school deemed Tim to be only trainable. Pat and I were devastated when we read the letter informing us that Tim was "Irreversibly mentally retarded."

Within days the words of a school psychologist deepened our grief. Our school superintendent, Bill Thompson, who is also a personal friend, invited us to his home. He arranged for the school psychologist, Mr. Smith, to be there to discuss recommendations for Tim's future schooling.

After introductions and the usual small talk, the conversation turned serious. Mr. Smith gave his opinion on where he felt Tim should be placed. We knew a regular classroom wouldn't work, but we were not prepared for what he was about to suggest.

He advised us to place Tim in an institution. He went on to explain that it would be for the benefit of our other two children. And what about Tim? If the letter informing us of Tim's retardation stunned us, we were doubly taken aback by this paralyzing suggestion. Our shocked reaction was piercingly visible.

That awkward discussion quickly turned around. Now we were hearing about a special education program about to get off the ground in Lake County and becoming available for kids like Tim. It would be modeled after a top-notch program already up and running in New York. Even though things were still in the planning and developing phase, Tim could be enrolled for the next school year, and that, we were to find out later, was Bush School in Libertyville.

What relief, but at the same time how disturbing. How could a school psychologist allow any child, but especially one from a close, loving family, to be put into an institution? As I talk to other parents of handicapped children, I now know that this suggestion was all too common, even up to recent years.

I pray you will keep that in the back of your mind as you continue to read this amazing story. Tim's life, with all its relationships and situations, was a shining example of outward and inward God-given characteristics that served him so well for thirty-eight years—and that the Creator of the universe doesn't say, "Oops, I've made a mistake." There is a reason and a purpose for those who go through life with the labels of "handicapped," "retarded," "impaired," and "disabled."

Where To Next?

The day of our mini-conference with Tim's teacher arrived, and she didn't beat around the bush or soften the blow. "Tim's behavior is abnormal!" We patiently listened to her describe how strange and controlled he was. We in turn defended our belief that discipline, which was part of Tim's upbringing, would continue. He wasn't treated any differently than his sister and brother.

It was sad how this woman who had experience with the handicapped did not believe they could be taught or trained. Our only experience was with our son. Were all mentally impaired children beyond help and unable to learn? Was this prevalent thinking used across the board for all children with special needs? We were not at all happy with this medieval approach.

Parents are in for a difficult life if their handicapped child is not disciplined. Some may have a tough time dealing with their child's abnormal condition. They may go through life blaming themselves and trying to make up for it with little reprimanding. Both parent and child suffer the consequences. We raised Tim with love and discipline, and he became a well-rounded, well-adjusted, happy child and adult.

Sometime later we learned Tim's teacher was the mother of a mentally retarded adult son. He had grown up during an era when access to facilities for people with mental and physical handicaps was nonexistent and family support of any kind unheard of. My heart went out to her, knowing that what was available for my son had not been there for hers.

We were surprised two years later when this same teacher—who not only looked sweet, she really was sweet—came to us and apologized for her narrow thinking. I know this was very difficult for her and I appreciated the fact that she felt a responsibility to do so.

She too was getting an education and turning away from the sincere belief that the retarded could not be taught. All of us were in this learning process together. We were going to discover how "special kids" could grow into respectable adults if they only have the means to better their lives like the rest of us.

Special People Are Here to Stay

Mental retardation means that the brain is not able to develop to its full potential. It is neither a mental disease nor mental illness. Learning disabilities vary from extremely low to close to normal. No two individuals are affected in the same way. Each child is unique. Each child is very, very special.

Before special education came into being, many handicapped children were hidden in their homes, some destined never to leave a particular room, attic, or basement. Many families kept their secret well concealed where even close friends would not have known a special child existed.

Thousands of retarded children and adults lived in institutions away from family contact. Parents who would visit their child early on would more than likely stop going altogether. It was terribly depressing. The parents, broken and grief-stricken, would then find it impossible to even speak the child's name.

Whatever potential these children could have reached would be terminated when separated from their family. One does not grow intellectually locked up in an abnormal environment. Later in this book I address a surprising discovery we made regarding this after Tim's graduation from special education when he was twenty-one.

In some situations, with the parents' permission, the state would take custody at birth of a physically or mentally crippled baby. These babies were considered a devastating burden on family and society. The child put into an institution would probably perish within a very short time. Others who lived longer lived lives of deprivation and loneliness.

They were special people, with hearts and souls, feelings and emotions. Families with nowhere else to turn were only left with hopelessness and despair. If a child were not taught how to feed himself, he would eat like an animal and most likely be treated as such. People were well meaning but totally ignorant. Unfortunately, this is the legacy of the handicapped living before and during the life of Tim Stagg.

Many children are born with perfect minds, but through no fault of their own are prisoners in bodies that cannot respond. All are capable of loving and being loved. Some were, and some still are, never given the chance to experience either.

A family with normal children would not have an inkling as to what was available for those with special needs. Chances are you might never meet a child who was retarded. We of course fell into that category.

So here we were embarking on a journey that had been laid out for us long before any of us were born. It was 1967, and doors that were once shut for the handicapped were now being opened. We were experiencing the dawn of a new era, and as it grew, we were to grow with it.

That first year at Bush School was a frustrating one. We didn't have bus service to our door, and Tim was dropped off two blocks from our house. I'll never forget one day as I watched for him after school. He walked down the street dressed in an assortment of disheveled play clothes that were put on him at school.

Instead of the teacher making sure he looked presentable when he left, Tim was allowed to leave that way. In my mind it was a way for her to let me know that something more was going on in the classroom during the day than just a place to be. I was furious. Tim was different and other children recognized this. Walking in a neighborhood dressed as he was put him in real jeopardy.

> KATHLEEN: I was painfully shy as a child, but if anyone made fun of Tim, I became a very protective and outspoken advocate for him. One memory out of many in regard to insensitive people was during a time I took Tim for a walk in our neighborhood. Tim was five and I was seven. He did not look any different from other children, but his problem became visible in the way he talked and walked. As we walked past some older kids on bikes, they started making fun of him. I ended up running to a neighbor's house who had to walk us home.

Enlightened Educators

Something unknown to us was about to be revealed. A new breed of educators specializing in all areas of the handicapped was graduating from our universities. The following year, newly trained special education teachers appeared on the scene, and students were separated into workable classes. As the new teaching concept was applied the contrast was astounding.

Along with Bush, other small vacant buildings located in countryside areas of Lake County were being utilized.

Grateful parents at long last, having been encouraged, were only too happy to send their youngsters to this newly formed SEDOL (Special Education Division of Lake County). Small yellow buses now dotted our highways, traveling long distances to pick up kids from every corner of the county.

Local school districts had to finance each child attending SEDOL. Now the school districts also needed to be educated. A large percentage of administrators did not feel SEDOL was necessary and balked at being forced to support an unproven and costly program.

There may have been some heated discussions that included cussin' in God's veins at the extra cost to our schools. The negative thinking didn't change overnight, but eventually SEDOL won them over. The program is an overwhelming success!

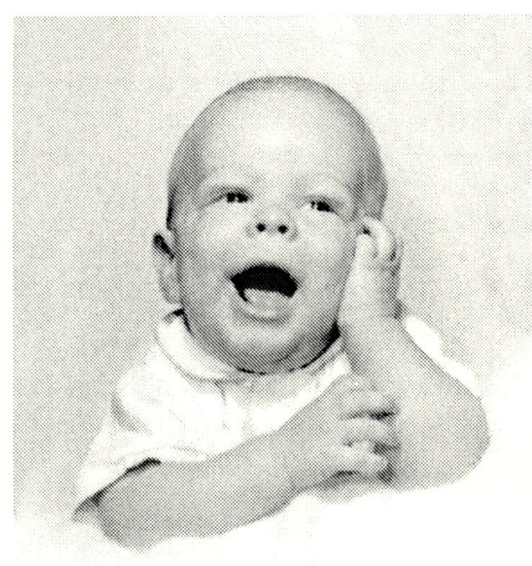

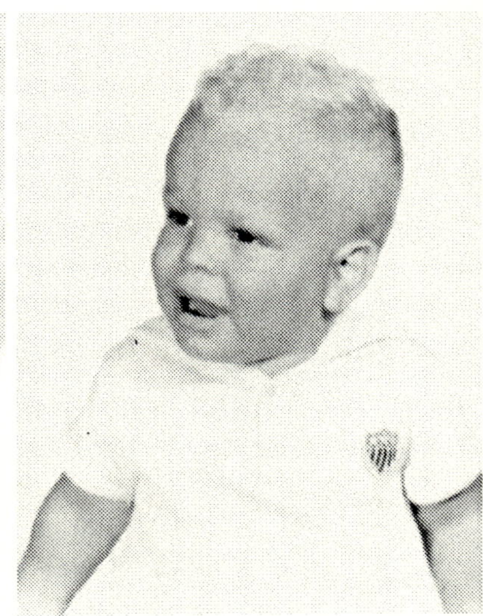

Three-months-old

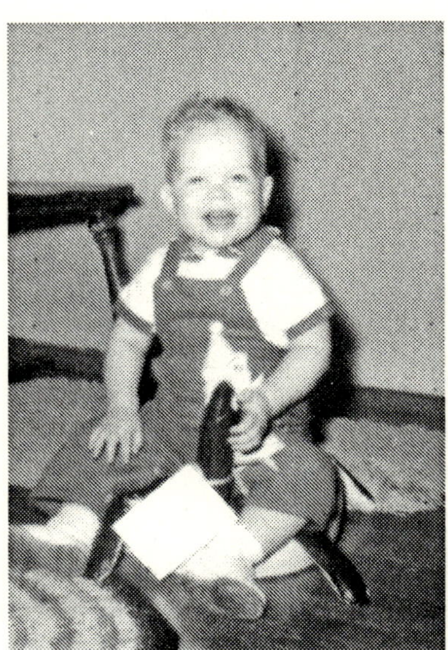

One-year-old

Halloween 1962

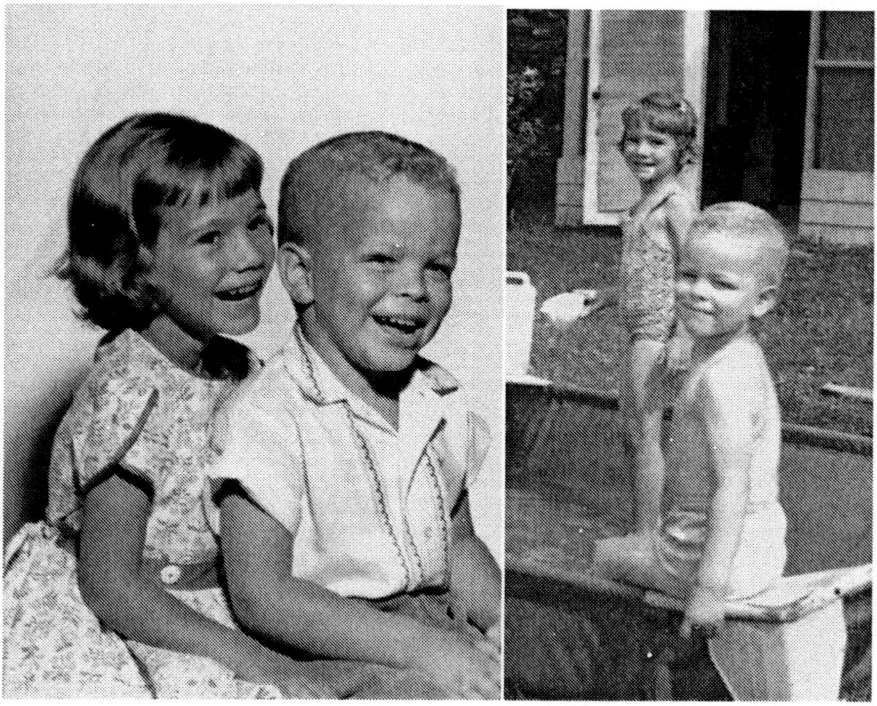

Kathleen (4 1/2), Tim (3)

Quinn & Tim

CHAPTER 3

Our Trusting Nature

Summer of 1969 when Tim was nine years old: An inner-city black child stayed with us for a week. At the end of the first day Tim said, "I like David, Mom, he's a lot of fun, and he has Afro-American parents, doesn't he?"

Let's look at that again. Sure enough we all saw it, Tim was walking with a limp. We were watching home movies of then five-year-old Tim. He and Quinn were holding hands walking away from the camera, and there was no denying it: he definitely had a limp. Now what?

Then in 1968 a well-known neurologist ordered testing to be done. They revealed Tim did not have brain damage, but rather a malfunction of the brain. It was discovered he was born with nerve endings inflamed and enlarged to the size of a pencil instead of being hair-thin. Our guess is that this was the cause of his not having reflexes and for the constant crying he did as a baby.

Congenital polyneuritis, for which there is no cure, was the diagnosis along with psychomotor retardation. Nerve conduction studies showed signs compatible with nerve degeneration. These were the nerves that supply the muscles. The neurologist prescribed a high dose of prednisone (a derivative of cortisone) to be taken for three months, and I don't remember asking why.

The horrors of cortisone were not known, and we trusted doctors and medications. Tim was on prednisone for just a couple of days when we watched with awe as he did forty knee bends at one time, and the day before he could not do one. We were elated as we watched him navigate stairs better. To us it was like a miracle.

This remarkable improvement was short-lived as our regular pediatrician, Dr. Walter Sulkowski, was not impressed. He immediately took Tim off the medication, which had to be done gradually. But by this time Tim had already showed one of its side effects, becoming moon-faced.

Questions regarding the wisdom of using prednisone will always haunt us. We may have lived with the miscalculation of that doctor, and Tim may have had undue hardships for the rest of his life because of it. Six months later, Tim's feet began turning inward, resembling clubfeet. In a very short time he had to crawl to get around, and it was at this time that Shriners Hospital for Crippled Children accepted him as a patient. After extensive examinations, leg braces were prescribed, which allowed him to walk before surgery had to be done.

Steroid medications (there are several) show other side effects along with weight gain in the face and body. There can be increased risk of infections and loss of calcium from bones, which can lead to osteoporosis. The list goes on, but I believe Tim's bones were affected.

At the age of nine, muscle transplants were performed on both feet. Again we learned something new. Children with neurological problems are known to mend slowly, so it wasn't a surprise to the doctors that the operation did not take.

At this point something else had to be done quickly or his feet would have gone beyond repair. So eighteen months after the muscle transplants, a more successful procedure was done with bone transplants. Both feet were fused at the ankle. Even though the fused ankles would no longer bend, Tim could walk.

Then slowly, ever so slowly, Tim's hips become permanently dislocated without our knowing it. This condition, along with the fused ankles, made his feet turn outward and his body swing from side to side with each step. Our learning experience was ongoing as we discovered how remarkable the body is and how amazingly it can adjust. Who would think one could walk with hips that weren't properly in their sockets? But the surgery on Tim's feet allowed him to walk with the use of a cane for 28 years.

During the numerous times Tim was hospitalized, Kathleen and Quinn sat for hours in the waiting room because they weren't allowed to be near any of the hospitalized children. Weeks and weekends stretched into years, and we discovered how an entire family is involved when one of them is disabled.

> KATHLEEN: I never felt our family was different from any other family even though we spent most of our weekends traveling to Chicago to see Tim during his many stays at Shriners Hospital. My younger brother Quinn and I had to find ways to entertain ourselves, along with those around us, while we sat for hours in the waiting room. We were not old enough to visit Tim in the dormitory-type room where all the boys were. At the end of the day we were allowed to wave to him from behind closed glass doors that looked down a long hallway.

Nutrition and Vitamins

During the eighteen months from muscle to bone transplants, one major change was made in Tim's diet: vitamins. We now knew that those with neurological problems have a harder time with healing. So after reading up on vitamins, we gave him vitamin C, calcium, magnesium, and zinc, known for their healing properties. His healing time after the second, more extensive surgery was as quick as someone who did not have a neurological problem. Vitamin E also played a big part in his being less nervous and a little less talkative.

There definitely had been a change for the good in his behavior. I discovered the healing elements of vitamins through trial and error, and they worked. We feel vitamins played a big role in why Tim did so well in all the surgeries and recoveries down through the years. Health-wise he excelled. The physical deformities were the daily struggle for him.

Friendships and Frustrations

It was no small education for all of us as Tim spent more and more time in the hospital. We had opportunities to see other hospitalized children and their families and grasp in minute ways what they were going through. We soon realized Tim was in much better shape than most.

These were the days when pregnant mothers were given thalidomide. It was a mild sedative used as a sleeping aid and it caused what came to be known as thalidomide babies. The condition is called phocomelia, a congenital deformity. One or both hands or feet are attached to the trunk by single, very short bones, giving them a flipperlike appearance. These beautiful children had perfect minds, but many had just a fingerlike projection from the shoulder or elbow.

One afternoon as Tim and I sat in the hospital clinic, a young mother came in pushing her daughter in a wheelchair. The child, around four years old, was exceptionally pretty with long, flowing brown hair. As her solemn-faced mother walked her to the desk, it took me a moment before I realized this beautiful little girl did not have arms or legs, only a head and torso. I still think about them after all these years and wonder what their lives were like and where that child might be today.

Untold hours were spent waiting. We waited in the clinic, waited in the hospital, waited for doctors, waited for X rays, waited for recoveries, waited for therapy, waited for braces, and waited for improvement. Tim's hospital stays were not just days, or even weeks, they were months at a time. Any child in a similar condition could look forward to the same. The medical staff is well known for the success they have in giving children the chance to live more normal lives, and the problems ran the full gamut of deformities from head to toe, to burn and accident victims.

Carlos Salazar was a young boy from Chicago who had surgery for clubbed feet. He and Tim became close buddies when they often found themselves hospitalized at the same time. The two of them created their own brand of medicine, which was a large dose of the giggles. Carlos's mother could not speak English, but for some reason, along with her son she took a liking to Tim. When Tim was about to leave Shriners after one of his operations, Mrs. Salazar baked him a beautifully decorated birthday cake to take home.

For a few weeks a seven-year-old boy with an angelic face was in the bed next to Tim. He had contracted spinal meningitis and all its dreaded side effects. He could not open his eyes or talk and had to be fed with a stomach tube. We and the staff talked to him with the hope he could hear us. I will always remember the sad, defeated expression from his loving grandfather who faithfully came to see him.

Friendships were made during hospital sojourns because Tim would see some of the same boys again as years came and went. One good-looking young man who we saw many times was paralyzed from the waist down after receiving the polio vaccine at the age of three. He was one of the unfortunate ones contracting the disease from the vaccine. About one in 2.4 million who are given the oral vaccine (OPV) actually contract polio. Today a safer method is recommended, which is given with an injection (IPV). Fernando had a wonderful, close family who encouraged him to look forward to college and a career.

Carlos Cabol Jr. was born with spina bifida. Many times he, too, called Shriners Hospital home at the same time Tim was there. The two of them became very close friends when they also found themselves classmates at Laremont School.

Through unbelievable situations, kids didn't complain. Our hearts went out to not only the youngsters, but their families as well. They suffered right along with them. Some children came from good homes, others did not, and you ached for those who never had visitors. When a child did not want to go home, you knew he was dealing with a terrible home life.

I recall a teenager who would rather stay at Shriners than go home. He had spina bifida and could not walk, being fully dependent on a caregiver. He would get very upset when it was time to leave and begged to stay at the hospital. It turned out his mother was an alcoholic, which created a nightmare situation for him when he was home.

One day a boy of fourteen came into the ward. His mother was angry and beside herself. He had been playing baseball with his friends when a teenage neighbor called him into his home. Reluctantly, the fourteen-year-old went into the house, but at the same time was distracted by the game he left outside. He was looking out the window when he heard a click. As he turned, he saw the teenager pointing a gun at him.

This time the gun went off and the bullet severed his spinal cord. He would never walk again. The teenager who shot him was not punished, claiming it was an accident, and continued his life as usual. The mother of the paralyzed boy was a school secretary, and every day she saw the boy who shot her son. The absolute anguish of this family cannot be grasped.

Yes, hospitals are eye-openers. They are also places of opportunity where minds and hearts reach out to God. Anyone with a handicapped child should spend some time in a hospital. Quickly they will find they are not alone and that the world is full of pain and sorrow.

I never said, "God, why me?" I looked around and saw terribly sad things happening to all kinds of people. I said, "God, why not me?" This was my feeling even before I was moved to look to His Son, Jesus, for my strength and comfort.

During this time, even though I felt "why not me?" I know I did not have inner peace and my body was straining to stay well. My negative attitude had me looking for the bad in everything, and I lived in constant fear. Getting through a day was almost impossible without lying down, and usually the dinner dishes didn't get done until the next morning because I was too exhausted to do them at night.

When Tim was 10, there was a suspicion of a brain tumor and he was sent to a Milwaukee hospital for a pneumoencephalogram, a terrible brain test that has been replaced by the CAT scan. Pat and I will never forget leaving him, which we were required to do, once he was settled in. He was in a large room all by himself with the test scheduled first thing in the morning.

Even as I write this, my heart has a sinking feeling. Tim was put into so many situations where he had to fend for himself. In spite of all the protection and care we were able to give, he was by himself during some very difficult circumstances. We left that hospital floor with tears in our eyes.

Tim, because he was so outgoing, said good-bye to us as he confidently walked into a room where there were three kids—complete strangers. We heard him introducing himself. What transpired after that we don't know. The next morning he had to deal with the dreadfully painful test and lay quietly for hours because of the after-effects. We were relieved to know he didn't have a tumor.

Tim only became more independent, braver, and more courageous during these times away from home. He was retarded but intelligent, and he would use what he knew to bluff his way through his daily encounters. His world revolved around television, and he memorized channels, times, and programs. He'd pick up a *TV Guide* and give anyone information on the programs for that day. Those around him did not know he couldn't read.

When Tim was older, the Christmas gift he looked forward to the most was a new calendar for the coming year and colored markers to mark off each day. His knowledge of days, dates, and time were of utmost importance in his daily routine and served him well for just about everything.

> QUINN: Tim always had a large calendar hanging on his wall, and he'd mark off each day. You could tell a lot of work went into this daily ritual as a bright color overlapped each square and sometimes worked its way onto the wall. Anyone who gave the present of a new calendar for Christmas knew it would make a big hit with him. It was something he could always count on for sure. Along with that cherished calendar would also be a new set of colored markers.

The Contribution of Television

Television is not my favorite medium. It has changed this country and it has changed the way families do things. The joy of communicating and being with one another—reading, playing games, and going places together—was given up for televised programs and sports events. Some longstanding traditions faced new challenges. Dinners were served in front of the tube, and the togetherness of parents and children was slowly being destroyed. Television became both entertainer and baby-sitter.

In Tim's case television was a learning tool. There was actually a positive side to TV. Imagine that! Gritting my teeth I learned to forego my feelings of irritation with the constant drone coming from his room. Then one day I realized—I wasn't paying attention to it anymore.

Years of watching and listening paid off. Tim gained great knowledge in just about everything and was up-to-date on world affairs, information he never would have acquired elsewhere. He'd keep us current with daily events and news-breaking stories, space flights and natural disasters. He knew important people and why they were well known.

Looking back, we probably did more with our children than most. My workaday world was in my home, so when all three kids returned at the end of the day, I was there. With all the operations and recuperation time in Tim's life, working outside the home was out of the question. The Lord blessed us with my not having to seek employment. Nor did I want to.

Evening meals were always together at the dining room table. It didn't matter whether we were dressed up or just wearing blue jeans (mostly blue jeans), dinner was served with candlelight. I wanted this time to be special and I wanted to see my children do the same when they had their families. Hot dogs and chips, or turkey dinners, candles would be flickering as we talked about everything together. Our lives were busy then, and families are even busier today. It's very important to set aside time for everyone to be together.

It's amazing how a child who didn't talk until he was four became so proficient in speaking. Tim was nine when my journaling began with the funny things he would come up with. His speaking skills excelled, and the words he used were correct, or nearly correct. He'd hear a word once and begin using it. With this gift of language, he developed into a real comedian and became well known for his contagious sense of humor.

My sister-in-law Sherry refers to those nearly correct words as "Tim-isms." Whenever she hears her granddaughter use words like "he's really hamsome," it's for sure a Tim-ism. Our lives were not dull because laughter was never far away for us. And to that I can still hear Tim reply with his usual "Correct amendo" or "I degree."

Pat received a couple of broken ribs from a head-on accident he was in when Tim was about eight. With a wave of his arm he questioned his dad, "Why didn't you beep the honk and tell him just to move on?" A coffee cake Pat was bringing home that morning did not survive the wreck, and Tim said he felt even more sorry for the coffee cake that got smashed.

It was obvious Pat was in a lot of pain and trying very hard not to laugh at the funny things Tim was telling him. Tim realized this when he saw how Pat would grimace, and he said, "I'm sorry, Dad." Pat, "Well, it's not your fault Tim." Tim, "I know—it's yours!"

In 1969, the astronauts took the orange drink Tang on their space flight. Naturally this was great advertisement for the company, one that was not lost by Tim. If the astronauts could drink Tang, we had to give it a try. One morning Kathleen let us know she really hated it. "Oh, Kathleen, just pretend you're on Mars," he snapped. Because she was his older sister, he probably felt she belonged on Mars.

> KATHLEEN: Tim was always very witty and usually came up with funny comebacks. For others this was funny but for me at times it was irritating. Tim was a mimic of my dad. Because my dad teased me all the time, Tim would always pipe in, and I would have two of them driving me crazy.

Tim definitely was perceptive. It's still hard to understand how his brain worked. On one hand he was not able to read, write, or dial a phone. On the other hand, the remarkable intelligence he possessed allowed him to be tuned in to most situations and react. He certainly did not lack self-esteem.

Earlier I described how the impact of Tim's personality upon us and others was bright and illuminating. Historically speaking, however, some of those illuminating times were delightfully brighter then he would have liked.

> MARK STEWART (son-in-law): Lead Bottom—yep, you read it right, ole' Lead Bottom as I would call him. Now you might feel I'm a little insensitive with regard to what Tim went through and all, but only he and I knew he was Lead Bottom. You'd kind of wonder how a guy who weighed 110 pounds soaking wet could get such a name. Well, just hold on a second and I'll tell you.
>
> Back in the late 70s before Tim's sister Kathleen and I got hitched, Tim had quite a week. To start the week out, three spokes on his wheelchair got broken and

nobody knew how he did it. And to this day no one ever will. I got wind of the broken spokes and teased him about maybe he was gaining a little too much weight. His reply to my declaration was, "Just be quiet Mark, I don't want to talk about it. Drop it." If you know me, I didn't drop it.

As the week went on, Tim somehow cracked his horse-head walking cane. Again, a few more fat jokes directed toward him weren't too warmly received. But we were buddies so he accepted the jesting. Then unbelievably a few days later Tim slipped while getting off the toilet and cracked the back holding tank and water went everywhere. And thus Lead Bottom was born.

Why Can't He Learn?

To look at Tim you wouldn't know he was retarded, so you expected more from him than he could produce. Each new school year, teachers tried to evaluate kids they were meeting for the first time. Every teacher, without fail, as they looked at Tim and heard him talk, felt he had the ability to really learn. The prospect of this was exciting and they would be anxious to see what he could do. But to their dismay, it would be no different than what we had discovered as parents. He simply was not able to perform. Socially he was dynamite, and this proved to be his most valuable asset.

Kathleen was twelve and quite indignant when she announced, "There's no reason Tim can't learn; no one is challenging him. I'm going to teach him to read." With that she set the chalkboard outside and arranged as close to a school setting as she could.

> KATHLEEN: I was absolutely sure Tim's teachers were wrong when they said he could not learn to read or write. I was in seventh grade when Quinn and I set up an entire classroom out in the yard. We had a desk, chalkboard, and beginning reading books. We tried over and over again to teach Tim the alphabet. It wasn't long, and all three of us ended up in tears because Tim truly couldn't understand. It was very difficult for me to accept.

Tim would go along with anything—to a point that is. Once the novelty wore off, that was it. And the novelty usually wore off in about ten minutes. Tim was intelligent enough to know what he could and could not do. He'd give it his best shot, and after that it wasn't important to him. He might color a picture but he couldn't put a puzzle together or play a board or card game. Not that he wouldn't make an effort to try, but he knew he couldn't do it, so within minutes it was all over.

As Kathleen began to work with Tim, she, for the first time, realized the frustration in trying to teach him to read. Like Tim, Kathleen too would give up her idea, and it was probably in the same amount of time. Ten minutes. At least that's what it seemed to me.

All of a sudden she ran into the house in tears. The reality had sunk in. Tim was Tim. He was different and nothing we did was going to change that. We could give him lots of love, encouragement, and a happy home. We would include him in all we did and he would grow socially. And really that was more important.

It was so much better for Tim to be able to talk well and to be around people, to be part of the everyday world and not have to read or write. In the end, Tim was much better off than so many other kids. He was happy and funny, and fun to be with. That day Kathleen learned what "special" meant in terms of who Tim was. It was good for her and it was good for Tim.

Questions like, "How old was I when I was a baby?" are typical for most kids. As Tim grew older his questions ran the full gamut; it was just that his age in relation to his questions was revealing. Our answers needed to be direct and uncomplicated. When still young he'd say, "Today I saw a wittle teesy E mouse" (meaning little teensy wee mouse). He grew and his vocabulary went through the roof.

When Kathleen was fourteen, she embroidered a wall hanging for our wedding anniversary that is still on our wall today. The title is "Heaven's Very Special Child":

Author Unknown

A meeting was held quite far from earth! "It's time again for another birth."

Said the angels to the Lord above, "This Special Child will need much love.

His progress may be very slow. Accomplishment he may not show.

And he'll require extra care from the folks he meets down there.

He may not run or laugh and play: his thoughts may seem quite far away.

In many ways he won't adapt and he'll be known as handicapped.

So let's be careful where he's sent we want his life to be content.

Please, Lord, find the parents who will do a special job for You.

They will not realize right away the leading role they're asked to play.

But with this child sent from above comes stronger faith and richer love.

And soon they'll know the privilege given in caring for their gift from heaven.

Their precious charge so meek and mild is Heaven's Very Special Child."

The Body—So Revealing

Scoliosis is the name for a curvature of the spine, and Tim developed a scoliosis of his upper back. Each year it was becoming worse. If his legs and feet were a problem, his deformed back attracted attention that much more.

Tim loved to swim, but we had to stop taking him to the community pool. Teenagers would whisper, point their fingers, and make fun of him. They ignored the fact that

Pat and I were there with him. We were saddened that the one thing he could do had to come to an end, as no one should be subjected to that kind of abuse. And surely as the sky is blue, Tim was very much aware of the kids and their remarks, and conscious of the way he looked and walked.

> QUINN: I remember how Tim always felt that he was more fortunate than others. He would often look at other kids who had physical problems much like his own, and he'd comment on how lucky he was, how he could have it worse.

The cross the handicapped bear is a great burden to them. Not only do they have their affliction to contend with (which for the most part they are acutely aware of) but also ignorant people, people who need to thank God for blessing them with healthy bodies and perfect minds.

No one knows what the future holds. One Sunday afternoon Pat took Tim, who was six, to a meeting held in our grade-school gym. People were talking and milling around, and as Pat talked to a friend he glanced at Tim and saw he was in trouble. Several boys had gone up to him with the remark, "What do we have here? Look, guys, a retard." Nothing more went beyond that remark as Pat came to Tim's rescue.

Several years later, we were sorry to learn that one of the boys had a younger sibling who developed serious physical problems, needing constant, lifelong attention. It's sad but true how this world has its way with cruel twists and turns. One turn in the road and we can find ourselves caught in its ugly grip.

Learning the Hard Way

As Tim grew, his spine began collapsing at a fast rate, even with the aid of a Milwaukee brace. This particular brace was designed specifically for him and went from hips to chin. Now it became clear something else had to be done as his rib cage overlapped his navel. If left uncorrected, his life span would be shortened.

At every turn in the course of Tim's life we asked doctors about the steroids he had taken when he was eight. We questioned whether it could have triggered the collapse of his feet and back. With one exception, all doctors have said that it was very probable.

Tim was fourteen when the decision was made to go ahead with an operation to straighten his back. Everything was explained to us, and we were prepared as much as we could be for a long duration. The repairing of his spine covered a seven-month period in the hospital with traction, surgery, and rehabilitation, and then continuing therapy when he returned home.

First was a month of traction to stretch his spine. A halo hoop encircled his head and pins were put through his knees to provide the stretching that was needed, and it worked. Halo hoops are readily used for head and spine injuries. Throughout his life, Tim was conscious of the scars left by the screws that went into his skull to hold the halo secure. He would brush his hair over the scars to hide them.

Finally, Tim's upper back was ready for the doctors to rebuild and fuse. Small pieces of bone taken from his ribs were used to stabilize the fusion. Pat and I stood next to the bed as Tim was coming out of the anesthesia, and we asked him how he felt. He replied softly, "I feel like a tight shoe." By that response we knew somewhat how he felt.

Down through the years, there were untold times when he wanted to express himself but couldn't find the right words. It amazed us how he'd create a verbal sketch to get his point across. He'd paint an oral picture—not unlike a form of animation—and what he wanted us to understand became crystal clear.

Remarkable Patience

Tim was on a circular rotating Stryker bed for months until doctors felt enough healing had taken place. This particular bed kept his body free from bedsores. He wasn't able to do anything but look at the ceiling or the floor, and could only hear the TV, but he never complained.

Two weeks after surgery, doctors planned to use pelvic bone to further strengthen the fusion. We decided enough was enough and didn't give them permission. The longer he was off his feet and not walking, the harder it would be to get him going again, which proved to be true when Tim finally got out of bed.

The surgeon had concentrated on Tim's troublesome back. Now this same surgeon stood in disbelief watching him take snail-paced steps. In an angry manner, maybe even cussin' in God's veins, he asked, "What on earth is wrong with him? What happened to him?" I know this doctor would have loved to see him leave his hospital bed and continue life as usual, especially with a newly repaired spine. But with Tim, nothing was easy, nor would it ever be.

When the pins in Tim's knees were removed, it was a surprise to find his knees had locked up and he was not able to bend them. There was an attempt to bend them surgically, but to no avail. So, to add to everything else, Tim could no longer bend his knees—forever! Tim's inability to bend his knees also affected the way he sat, and that too became a lifetime problem. In spite of it all, we saw a blessing. When Tim reached five feet, he stopped growing.

Sometimes professional decisions are seen through a narrow tunnel focusing only in the area of expertise. All aspects of a person should be addressed, especially for one dealing with so many different problems. Tim's fusion was a success inasmuch as it stabilized his spine for many years, but as he grew older the scoliosis slowly worsened.

That Tim was short was fortunate for all of us. With not being able to bend his knees, if he was one inch longer he would not have been able to get out of a chair by himself, get in or out of a car, or sit on our toilet. It also would have been impossible for us to carry him up and down stairs as we did. And because sitting to eat was not comfortable for him, he preferred to stand at our kitchen counter to eat his meals.

When we look at all the negative things in Tim's life, we also see parallel blessings that were positive. So we can either go through life with our glass half-empty or half-full. Looking for all the things to be thankful for helped us through some terribly difficult and demanding times.

The final diagnosis: Tim had Charcot Marie Tooth disease. This was the same diagnosis given him when he was six years old when they noted he had the characteristics of Charcot Marie Tooth (peroneal muscular atrophy). However, it usually runs in a family, and we had no familial history of any similar condition. It was during a clinic visit when a doctor from Shriners looked at Tim and just shook his head and sighed. When I asked what was wrong, he said, "I've never seen one child with so many different things wrong."

We were also told that his heart, which is a muscle, would be adversely affected by his condition and that his life would be shortened because of it. From then on we lived with the fear we could lose him at any time. Later another doctor said Tim should live a normal life. However, in the back of our minds, "the heart being a muscle" would always nag us.

> QUINN: I remember taking Tim trick-or-treating on Halloween. We would start off walking with several friends, but soon we were walking alone because Tim could not keep up and no one was willing to wait for us.
>
> The neighborhood where we lived had a lot of hills, and many homes had stairs going down to them. Tim had a hard time going up and down stairs, so when we reached those houses, Tim would wait on the street above and I would take his treat bag along with mine to the door. I can still remember how some people would make crude comments and only put candy in

one bag and not the other. This happened even when they could see Tim standing in the distance.

Then there were those folks who would put candy in both bags but would make me feel like I had just scammed them out of something. Tim never knew about the comments or that candy was put in only one bag. I remember thinking to myself how strange people can be over such a small thing.

Christmas 1967 in new "old" house

Recovering with Mrs. Salazar's birthday cake

The only one to catch a Lake Trout

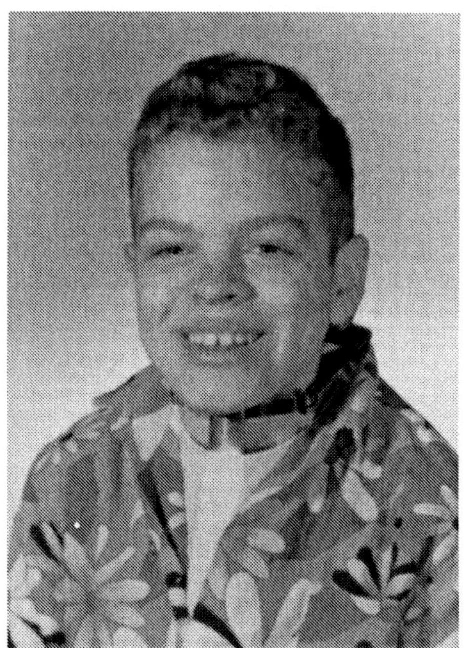

Tim (13) wearing Milwaukee Brace

CHAPTER 4

Jerry Lewis Meets Tim Stagg

A friend of ours was celebrating his birthday and as usual was asked how old he was. He jokingly answered that he was only thirty-nine. After a momentary pause, Tim replied, "You know, Jack Benny died at thirty-nine." The difference was that Tim wasn't joking.

Naps during the middle of the day were very helpful, and I took advantage of this privilege whenever possible. They were rejuvenating, raising my energy level to get me through the evening hours feeling good.

On this particular afternoon, I was sleeping in the bed next to Tim when I heard a pounding sound. Looking up I saw Tim's arm hitting the wall and by the movement of his body I thought he was dying. His eyes were closed and he could not hear me as I kept screaming out his name. Not wanting to leave him alone, I put him on the floor and dragged him to the phone.

The ambulance rushed him to the hospital, and tests showed he'd had a grand mal epileptic seizure. It must have been seizures that caused the recent falls he had. After spending the night, medication was given and he returned home, but effects of the seizure left him exhausted.

A special picnic had been planned for the following day at the Kitchens of Sara Lee in Deerfield, Illinois, a company known for its pies, pastries, and assorted desserts. Tim was still feeling weak from the ordeal, and we wondered if he would be strong enough to attend. It was May 14, 1977. Gail Ranker, close friend and neighbor, and secretary to Sara Lee's vice president, Tom Barnum, got permission to invite Tim. Sara Lee was sponsoring this special Craft Fair for the Muscular Dystrophy Association, and Gail knew Jerry Lewis was going to be there. It was to be a surprise for Tim, now seventeen, so he wouldn't become too excited in anticipation.

The day was perfect for a picnic—warm and sunny. Sara Lee's beautiful landscape was an awesome sight, beginning with the carpet of green grass, lots of trees, flowers, and well-manicured bushes. Brightly colored balloons were everywhere, providing a cheerful, festive mood. Employees of Sara Lee were busy with activities planned for the day, which included serving box lunches to everyone. Children and adults with muscular dystrophy, most in wheelchairs, were spread out over this large expanse of green.

Tim was given his box lunch, and after taking a bite of his sandwich an announcement came over the loudspeaker that Jerry Lewis just arrived. At that moment it was as though

Tim had become electrified. He could not contain his excitement. He put down his ham sandwich and that was the end of lunch. We didn't have time to think because all of a sudden a Sara Lee representative took hold of Tim's wheelchair and off they went to find Jerry.

When Tim saw Jerry in the distance, he began calling and waving to get his attention. Tim considered Jerry his good buddy. Why not? Didn't he see Jerry on TV and follow his movies? Didn't he watch the MD Telethon faithfully every year? Didn't he just love the guy? Yes, indeed, Jerry was a good friend whether Jerry knew it or not.

The next thing we knew, Jerry was approaching Tim as though they were old lost friends, and there was an immediate bond between them. Jerry quickly found out that he had a best friend and his name was Tim Stagg from Lake Villa, Illinois.

The events of that afternoon are indelibly etched in our minds. Because Tim was so quick in making conversation and quips, the dialog between him and Jerry was unbelievable. It was the equivalent of a rehearsed stage act—one-on-one and hilarious. Tim had Jerry and everyone else in earshot in stitches from laughter.

What a priceless expression we all received from Mr. Lewis when Tim looked up and asked, "Hey Jerry, how's Dean Martin?" Dean and Jerry had split up long ago (1955), so the unexpected question created a delightfully funny reaction. Jerry Lewis and Dean Martin became well-known for their humorous talent on stage, in films, and on television. It began in the early 1950s when Pat and I were in high school. Their popularity went off the charts, and I guess you could say that we, too, grew up with Jerry Lewis.

Then Jerry took Tim's cane and used it like a golf club as they continued exchanging barbs and poking fun at one another. Jerry gave Tim a hard time about his Chicago Cubs baseball cap (he never went anywhere without it). So the humor turned to the rivalry between the Cubs and Los Angeles Dodgers.

Those manning the cameras kept the film rolling for both video and still shots that were given to us at a later date. With all the attention Tim received, we began to move him to the back of the crowd. We didn't want to monopolize Jerry's time because kids and adults with muscular dystrophy are not able to express themselves as forcefully as Tim could. They needed to interact with Jerry as well.

The huge crowd had assembled around the cutting of an enormous clown cake. As we continued to stay in the background, we saw Jerry stretching his neck, looking out over the crowd. He spotted us and motioned for us to come closer, and then he walked toward us, meeting us halfway.

Jerry brought a piece of cake and gave it to Tim. We felt humbled and honored at the same time. He began asking questions, and we explained as best we could about Tim's complicated problems. It was a privilege to have Jerry so interested. We talked and he listened, and the seriousness of his expression showed genuine concern. Then the unbelievable happened. Jerry asked us if we would bring Tim to Las Vegas for the 1977 Muscular Dystrophy Telethon that coming September.

We were awestruck. All eyes were upon us as the throng of children and adults completely encircled the four of us. With our heads in a fog, we accepted this once-in-a-lifetime invitation. The most natural thing for Pat was to ask if Jerry might just be kidding around. "I don't kid about things like this," Jerry replied. "All the arrangements will be made for you, and I'll be calling you in a week."

Gail Ranker in the meantime was beside herself. She was thrilled that Tim was having such a fantastic time. She stood alongside us grinning from ear to ear, and in a moment of craziness, Jerry turned around, wrapped his arms around her, and kissed her. She was shocked, and also never again to live down his comment, "I'll give the old broad a thrill." For many years, Tim would have a good laugh along with the rest of us, as we reminded Gail of her encounter with Jerry Lewis. And it goes without saying that the Irish have a great sense of humor, and Gail with her wit and loveable personality heads the list. It couldn't have happened to a better person.

When MDA representatives realized Tim would be going to the telethon, they were scratching their heads and asking, "Who is this kid?" They had never heard of Tim Stagg, and this could become quite a sticky problem for them. Someone invited to the Telethon and he doesn't have muscular dystrophy? So now the question was who is he and what are his physical problems?

We gathered up Tim's balloons and souvenirs and were ready to head for home. It was a storybook day—one we would never forget. As we were about to leave, two MD reps came up to us and asked what Tim's diagnosis was. And the answer to their inquiry was the one Shriners Hospital gave us. Tim had Charcot Marie Tooth disease. To our surprise and to their relief, they told us Charcot Marie Tooth fell into the category of muscular dystrophy. Whew! What an amazing revelation!

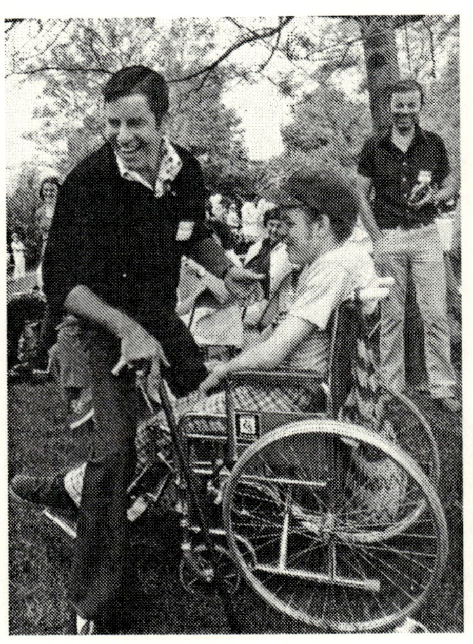

Jerry & Tim exchanging barbs

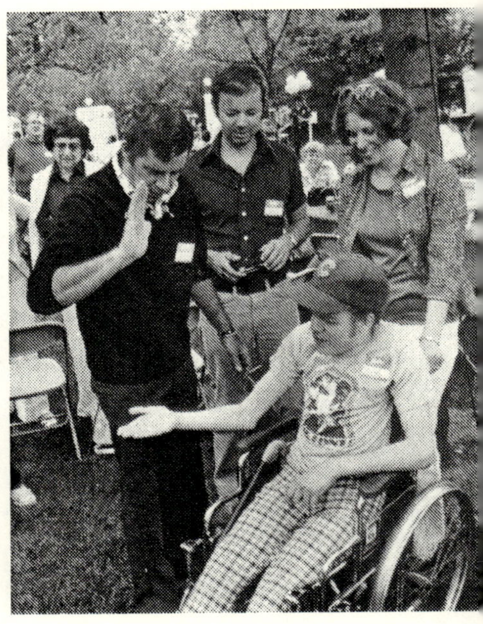

Gimme five!

Gayle Ranker

Something to smile about

Photos Courtesy of the Muscular Dystrophy Association

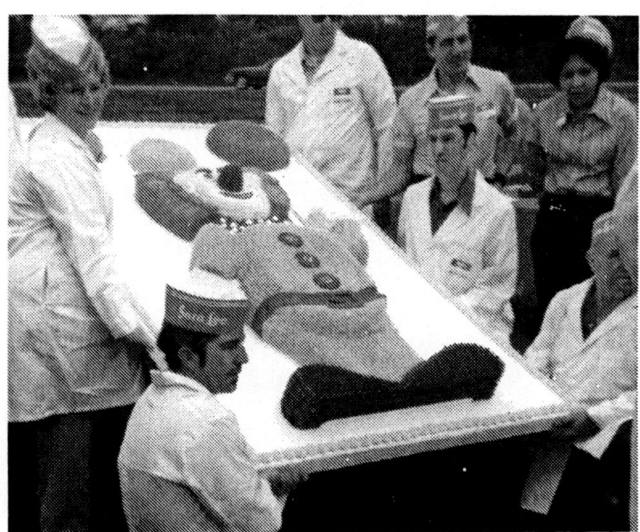

Sara Lee's huge clown cake

An Exciting Adventure

"Hi Patti, Jerry here, you guys still coming to Vegas?" It was a week after the picnic, a Saturday morning, and Jerry was calling us from California. I responded as well as I could and gave the phone to Pat and Tim. Jerry Lewis calling us? This was incredible.

How did all this happen? Never in a million years would we begin to look for something like this; the Lord just laid it in our laps. It was a thrill, but most of all it was a blessing. Yes, it was a blessing because nothing happens in our lives only by coincidence. God has a master plan and no one gets overlooked. So yes, indeed, this was a blessing.

Arrangements for the trip were being made. Our contact person from MDA was a wonderful man by the name of Jim Tillman, who himself had muscular dystrophy. From May until September, Tim had much to think about and anticipate—he was going to the Telethon.

The headline in our local newspaper on August 11, along with article and two pictures of Tim and Jerry read, "Tim Stagg To Appear In Jerry Lewis Telethon."

The long-awaited September day arrived. It was sunny and beautiful, and relatives, neighbors, and friends were at our home to see us off. In addition to the activity all around us, the Waukegan News Sun sent a reporter to get pictures. Pretty soon a limousine pulled into our driveway to take us to O'Hare Airport in Chicago. Tim and I had never flown before, and a lot of firsts were awaiting us in this amazing adventure. When we landed in Las Vegas we were met by a naval escort and driven to the Sahara Hotel.

We didn't know if Tim would actually be seen on national TV, so everyone back home watched till their eyes popped. He sat within reach of Jerry, Ed McMahon, and all the well-known entertainers such as Johnny Carson, Frank Sinatra, Tony Bennet, Robert Goulet, Carol Lawrence, Englebert Humperdinck, and the impressive list goes on. My sister Sharon and I were in grade school with Ann Margaret in Fox Lake, Illinois, so we also took in her show.

Pat recalls how Tim had to go to the washroom, and as they were moving in that direction, Jerry and Ed McMahon hurried over to them. Jerry wanted Ed to meet Tim. I'm sure Jerry was taken aback as Tim informed him, "I can't talk now, Jerry. I have to go to the john."

Tim never got on television, and it's just as well. If he were asked any questions or asked to give a statement I would be holding my breath with horror, not knowing what he'd say. Quinn, at home, did record for us the moment Jerry told Tom Barnum over the national network how Tim Stagg was right there with them for the entire Telethon.

Local stations in Las Vegas had their own promoters. They'd get people to go outside during the Telethon for their own filming. Someone from this local station told us Jerry Lewis comes out to the poolside at a particular time. It sounded great to us, so we went outside.

A good number of people were gathered around the pool, and we joined them expectantly. Then a news reporter asked if we'd mind being on local TV. And when we agreed, with mike in hand, he began asking questions directly to Tim.

Tim answered each question perfectly, and I was really happy it had gone so well.

We assumed that was the final take, but quickly discovered it was only a rehearsal. Now a rush of fear came over me. I knew what Tim had said the first time around would never come out the same once the show was broadcast live. And that's exactly what happened. Normally he could carry on a regular conversation without a problem till the cows come home. But when put into a situation where he needed to make a statement or respond to questioning that required a direct answer—well, that changed things. To us it was a disaster—for that poor reporter a disaster. I wonder if he was silently cussin' in God's veins?

Twenty years later during a high school reunion, we met a graduate friend who lived in Orange, California. Jack Hingst and his wife Jean were watching the Telethon on their local station. He recognized Pat and me and heard the infamous interview. Jack's life was deeply touched that day, not by what Tim said, but because Tim had muscular dystrophy. When we did see Jack, it was difficult for him to talk about Tim without his eyes filling with tears. Another coincidence? I don't think so.

When we were at the Telethon, we met Matt Brown, poster child for 1977, and his parents. His mother told us a touching story about Jerry Lewis—a story that normally does not get told.

Matt had become dangerously ill, and his parents knew he might not make it through the crisis. She explained how Jerry flew from California to Georgia to be with Matt.

Through his encouraging words and upbeat presence, Jerry was able to turn the momentum, and Matt recovered. His mother couldn't say enough about Jerry's genuine caring and love for kids like Matt and Tim. In 1998, twenty years later, *Quest* magazine published a book review on an autobiography written by Matt called *Crying in the Night.*

Summer Camp

Now that Tim was on the MD roster, all kinds of doors were opened to him. After attending the Sara Lee picnic in May, we didn't know what great things lay ahead, such as their summer camp in June. Father's Day was the date set for camp to begin, and it was quickly approaching.

This yearly event was held at the YMCA Camp Hastings in Lake Villa, ten minutes from our home. Organization of volunteers, campers (MD patients), food, activities, medical personnel, supplies, and guest performers had been under way months in advance.

Immediately after the picnic, Sue Rudolph from the Chicago office called and invited Tim to camp. She assured us he would be well cared for as campers are provided a volunteer one-on-one. Tim had never been to any camp, and Pat and I hesitated about whether we should let him go. It was a difficult decision but with Sue's encouragement and reassurance, plans were made for him to attend.

Tim was extremely nervous as we left our house that Father's Day. His bags were bulging with the clothes and supplies he would need for a week. We drove onto the dusty road and up to the parking area. Looking past the railed fence we saw a large grassy area with a basketball court. It was full of assorted colors, moving and blending into a picture of activity and fun. The summer breeze carried with it voices and sounds that made you want to join in.

Once Tim was registered, we immediately found ourselves surrounded by happy, energetic volunteers. We were made to feel so welcomed—even the sense of feeling loved, which might be hard to understand. After we met the doctor and nurses we were on our way to the assigned cabin. There we met Tony Mineo, Tim's volunteer for the week. Tony and his brother Tim were first-time volunteers that year, and they made Tim's first camp experience an unforgettable one.

The people and the fun, the recreation and the laughter, and the lifelong friendships that burst into Tim's life are history. He came home a new person, exhausted from a week of entertainment, crafts, dancing, bonfires, dates, hilarity, and dozens of new friends. He slept for two full days.

There were as many camp stories as mosquito bites. He got married several times to some nifty nurses and stayed up late at night over lingering fires. He brought home his first stick house that would become a yearly tradition, each one a different size, shape, and color. He sang songs and had fun joking with others, and laughed his hearty laugh that has remained tucked in the hearts of those who came to love him. He danced his legs off and swam in the pool. One of the kids who worked in the kitchen was a fellow student at Laremont School and the Y had provided a summer job for him.

Lively Encounters and Dancin' Feet

MDs yearly camp became the catalyst for opening doors, and once again, an avenue for more growth entered into Tim's life. Attending camp became the highlight of his year from then on. His remark after one of those busy weeks was "At the end of camp we're all crazy happy" (meaning slap-happy).

Making new friends was a wonderful accomplishment in the life of a young man with many different physical handicaps. Most importantly, he was also mentally handicapped and would not totally understand all the jargon and jokes and instructions. It would be amazing if he had endeared himself to everyone, but I know that is not being realistic. Personalities are so different; some work together and some do not. Conflicts and misunderstandings are a part of being involved with people, and I'm sure it was the same for Tim as for any of us.

In spite of this, Tim used so abundantly what God had given him so abundantly: the gifts of speaking well and a great sense of humor, part of the legacy Tim left for those who befriended him. We hear repeated time and time again those same sentiments from a large number of men and women who knew him. I cannot emphasize enough how this and so much more had wrapped itself around the life of a young person who could have spent a lifetime lost in an institution.

In 1992, MDA could no longer continue the camping program for people over eighteen. The Association of Horizon, a program already in existence for handicapped adults, took over the yearly camp for MD patients. Horizon provides camp with the same high standards as the Muscular Dystrophy Association, and some volunteers donate time to both organizations.

The men and women who work with children and adults dealing with neuromuscular diseases deserve our respect and praise. Knowing how badly they are needed at camp, they rearrange their regular schedules with family and jobs to be there. Throughout the year, untold hours are spent behind the scenes organizing every detail. We cannot say enough "thanks" to all the people involved. Horizon also provides yearly events for camp friends to keep in touch.

All in all, Tim enjoyed camping experiences for twenty years, and during this time he came to be known as "Dancin' Machine Stagg." He was one of the few people with MD who could walk (with a cane) and dance. And dance he did!

He held his cane straight out in front of him with both hands and swung it back and forth and in circles, keeping time to the music. How he never lost his balance or tumbled down, I don't know. A wheelchair was used only when Tim would have to walk a long distance and for the ability to sit comfortably.

Tim returned home from one of his camping weeks and told us, "They named a dance after me, and it's called 'The Stagg.'" Tim was known for lifting the spirits of those around him, and we were told many times how he got things going at camp when the mood was down and needed some life.

Often it was "The Stagg" that ushered in the evening's activities with Tim leading the festivities. So at camp he became for them, what he was to us: sunshine on their shoulders.

> MARK: Tim used to go to a special camp for disabled kids close to our home in Lake Villa. His parents would take a much-needed vacation the same week as camp. Tim's brother Quinn and I were working together when Tim called and told him it was parents' night the next day. "Since Mom and Dad are gone, could you and Mark come after work for dinner for parents' night?"
>
> Well, of course we went. But we didn't realize ole' Lead Bottom had pulled another one of his fast ones on us till we walked into the mess hall and were greeted by curious counselors as to why we were there. The expressions and puzzled smiles on their faces told us immediately, "We had been had by Tim." Who, by the way, couldn't wait to introduce us to his counselors, the nurses, the cooks, the babes from last night's T-shirt contest, his date from the night before—you get the picture. Tim kind of ran the joint, as he would say.

Visual Insight That Few See

When we dropped Tim off at camp back in 1977, we experienced another first to be added to the lifelong string of eye-openers. We saw the effects of what muscular dystrophy does to the young and old. There was a young man in the fetal position who had arms and legs that were not much larger around than a broom handle. His body had atrophied to where he fit on a rather small rectangular board. And that's how his caregivers transported him around.

Through the years, Tim shared cabins with men who needed oxygen around the clock as well as special beds and equipment. The family, Muscular Dystrophy Association, and Association of Horizon provide everything necessary for them to be away from home for a week. No matter what condition some of these "campers" are in, this week is the highlight of their year too. They will be around loving, caring people. They will enjoy the laughter and music and good friends. They will have something to think about for the rest of the year—good memories that surface over and over again as they deal with the struggles of every day. And then they can always look forward to next year's camp.

Every year brought news of a former camper who had died. They had passed from this earthly world to the world that awaits all of us where there is no more pain or tears, and those who have muscular dystrophy live with both and a whole lot more. In the Bible, Revelation 7:17 says, "For the Lamb [Jesus] at the center of the throne will be their shepherd; He will lead them to springs of living water. And God will wipe away every tear from their eyes."

As I look back, we probably never would have discovered that Charcot Marie Tooth was part of the muscular dystrophy family. If it weren't for Jerry clowning around with Tim—or was it the other way around—we would have left that picnic with wonderful memories of a great day. However, the fact that Jerry asked us to bring Tim to Las Vegas opened unbelievable opportunities. What we expected to be merely a great picnic turned out to be a lifetime of blessings.

Chances are the Muscular Dystrophy Association never would have become part of Tim's life. But no, it was not just luck, it was part of a plan—God's plan. I've come to believe things don't just happen. It's not just a coincidence that Tim was invited to be at the Sara Lee outing that day. Nor was it a coincidence that Jerry Lewis was there. It wasn't a coincidence that Tim returned home from the hospital when he could just as well have stayed an extra day or been too weak to go.

Romans 8:28 tells us, "And we know that in all things God works for the good of those who love Him, who have been called according to His purpose." And I know God felt it was very good that Tim met Jerry Lewis.

A year later Jerry made another appearance in Chicago at Brunswick, the company that makes bowling and sports equipment. Again Tim was invited, and those in wheelchairs were lined up awaiting Jerry's arrival. It was another beautiful, sunny day. I'd like to think that the sun shines on both Jerry and his kids, and this too is no coincidence.

Jerry and his entourage arrived. As he moved toward the row of wheelchairs he pointed straight at Tim and said to those with him, "Look who's here." He walked directly to Tim, shook his hand, and talked to him.

The Blue Balloon

On September 8, 1982, I wrote a letter to Wally Phillips, who had a morning radio program on WGN in Chicago.

> Dear Wally: One Thursday you were talking about messages being sent attached to balloons. I would like

to share the following experience we had to give you an idea how far balloons can travel.

In June 1979, our son Tim, who was 19, was spending his last morning at the MDA camp. It was held at Camp Ravenswood (Ravenswood and Hastings are back-to-back) in Lake Villa, when all the kids sent balloons off with their names and addresses attached. This was Friday, June 25.

By the following Friday, Tim received a postcard from the Joe Rufener family in Sterling, Ohio, 400 miles away. Their 14-year-old son Lyle, who worked on a dairy farm, found the balloon in the field. They thought someone had thrown it out of a passing car and were surprised to find it did indeed travel all those miles. The Rufeners sent the tag (with traces of manure from the field) and balloon back to Tim so he could save it. We continue to correspond with this wonderful family of seven.

As long as I'm writing, I'd like to add that this balloon experience happened because of the great camp my son is able to attend every year. He also goes to an MD clinic at Evanston Hospital where top specialists give of their time. Both camp and clinic are free of any cost to us. The services and equipment that muscular dystrophy patients receive are all free of any charge. We know personally that the money does indeed go where it is needed most. We cannot say enough on how thankful we are that it is available for Tim. Most sincerely . . .

A letter from Lyle Rufener followed the postcard. It read: "Dear Tim, I thought you might like to have your balloon back for a souvenir. It might be a little dirty from landing in the cornfield—probably even might have a little cow manure from Ohio. It wasn't even broken when I found it, but it kept getting smaller and smaller as it was setting around the house. . . ."

We still hear from the Rufener family each Christmas. They were kind to Tim, sending him gifts and letters. And in April of '91, Lyle paid us a visit. We called our local newspaper and filled them in on what we thought would be a good human-interest story. They thought so too. A reporter took pictures of Lyle and Tim together and wrote about the above heartwarming story. It made the front page.

One of those nifty camp nurses

Camp is sooo much fun!

Good friend & camp helper, John Driscoll

Lyle Rufener from Sterling, Ohio, & Tim
make front page of local paper

CHAPTER 5

Logic With Discernment

Dinnertime grace once given by Tim: "Name of the Father, Son and Holy Ghost. Oops, I mean Holy Spirit, we'll say Ghost on Halloween."

Television provided Tim the entertainment of watching sports. The Chicago Cubs topped the list. He was a true-blue baseball fan, win or lose. Just for fun we used to kid him about "his friend" Harry Caray, who at that time was the announcer for the Chicago White Sox. Tim would have a fit. He made it very clear that there was no way he would ever be Harry's friend. He considered the Sox and Harry the enemy, part of the rivalry between the two Chicago teams.

Then the unthinkable happened. Harry went to work for the Cubs. Lo and behold, Tim couldn't say enough about this great American and Cubs announcer Harry Caray. He'd sing with gusto at the seventh-inning stretch when Harry would belt out, "Take Me Out to the Ball Game." As the National Anthem was sung at the beginning of each game, Tim would stand in his room, place his hand over his heart, and join the crowd in the Wrigley stands.

> MARK: Tim was just fun to be around. The things he would come up with, not even trying to be funny, would kill you with laughter. Just ask his mom about the "far—ng" dog story while on vacation. Or the time Tim's Aunt Anna Mae and Uncle Bob, beaming with pride, bought him a beautiful and expensive Chicago White Sox warm-up jacket, the ultimate present for "Mr. Baseball Fan."

One day my cousin Anna Mae and husband Bob Conrad came to visit. It was Aunt Anna Mae and Uncle Bob to Tim, and both were very dear to him. They in turn had a special place in their hearts for Tim. As usual they brought a gift for their favorite buddy.

Tim always enjoyed getting presents—they didn't have to be big or expensive. He quickly unwrapped the brightly covered box and lifted the lid. Without a word or a moment of hesitation, he placed the lid back on, slid the box back to Anna Mae and matter-of-factly let them know, "I don't like the Sox!"

In a flash they discovered that Tim didn't waste time with details. He wasn't impressed with the beautiful Sox jacket and would rather not have anything at all than to receive something with Sox on it. He was always direct and honest, and this story is still talked about. Needless to say the jacket was replaced with one from Chicago's northside team.

> MARK: Tim's famous words still echo in my head, "The Sox stink, the Cubs don't." If anyone wanted to get a rise in him, all they'd have to do is tease him about liking the Sox and he'd really get ticked off.

> QUINN: For Tim's thirty-sixth birthday, someone bought him a Sox helmet. It was glossy black with white letters. After the initial shock, he braced himself, tightened his face, and actually let Mark put it on his head. As fast as it went on, it came off, and the flash of a camera gave us a priceless photo. Everyone had a great laugh, and Tim even let out a few chuckles himself along with a warning or two.

Tim's bedroom was centrally located in our home. He could watch TV or listen to music and still know what was going on in the rest of the house. He'd wander to where we were, put in his two cents, and then retreat back to his room.

Later that evening Bob, Anna Mae, Pat, and I sat talking around a relaxing fire. Bob turned to me and made the comment, "Tim is truly the light of your life, isn't he, Patti?" And naturally I agreed with a prompt, "Yes, he really is." Several minutes passed as we continued to talk, when Tim poked his head into the room and said, "Hey Mom, the light of your life is ready to go to bed." Instantly our fireside conversation turned into roaring laughter, compliments of Tim.

> MARK: Yeah, Tim and I had a lot of fun, but on two occasions Raquel, as I fondly call my mother-in-law,

wasn't so amused. One day Tim and I were outside standing by the old pop-up camper when a bird flew over and dropped his white bird doodoo on the top. Tim and I looked at it, then at each other and I said, "The white bird doodoo tastes like powdered sugar." End of discussion—so I thought.

Two weeks later I get a phone call from Raquel, but really a mad Patti, asking if I had told Tim that bird doodoo tastes like powered sugar? I confessed and we both died laughing as she told me how she and Tim were sitting outside having lemonade when a bird deposited some of his "powdered sugar." Tim, not missing a beat, swiped it up with his finger and popped it into his mouth. We both got in trouble that day.

The good fortune—or should I say the great blessing?—of having a special child is that they turn into special adults. Our lives were full of loving companionship. The element called the generation gap that sometimes gets in the way of parent-child relationships was nonexistent.

As an example of how our lives were brightened by a special young man of twenty-one, Tim told me, "I'm going to bring home a flower for you for Mother's Day. It'll be wrapped up, but I can't tell you about it."

Our home isn't too big, and Tim was always in hearing range. We could never be in the house that he didn't know exactly where we were. Sometimes it was annoying, but we needed to remind ourselves how much he depended upon us and how important it was for him to feel secure. He couldn't climb stairs, and our bedroom is on the second floor. But if Tim didn't know I was there, in a very short time I'd hear him at the bottom of the stairs. Then he would call out, "Are you up there, Mom?" How I yearn to hear those words again.

"What's for lunch?" Or if it was the weekend, "What's for dunch?" This was Tim's expression for lunch and dinner. Breakfast dishes weren't cleared, and I'd hear that awful question. Tim loved people and his privacy; television and music; and especially, he loved to eat. His world revolved around a limited sphere, and simple things were treasures. I love to eat, too, so I needed to cook, but I'd rather be reading a book—or scrubbing the floor. Cooking is not my favorite job. Tim's question, "What's to eat?" was like someone stepping on a sore toe.

If Tim was trying to talk to me and I seemed miles away and not responding quick enough, I'd hear, "Earth to Mom, Earth to Mom." He was part of everything we did, and we were drawn into all things that were interesting to him. Every detail of our lives was an open book, and we never had any secrets with Tim around. If we'd overlook him in a situation or conversation, we'd hear, "Hey, what am I, chopped liver?" It has been hinted that many tales were told at school that we will never know about, and I think it's better that we don't.

> MARK: Some time after the powdered sugar episode, Tim and I were alone and a mosquito landed on my arm. Tim watched as I proceeded to whack it and pretend to pop it into my mouth. Tim just sat there for a minute, his curiosity getting the best of him, and he asked, "What do mosquitoes taste like?" I told him, "Chicken." End of discussion.

You guessed it. Tim replayed the whole scenario in front of his mom, explaining that mosquitoes taste pretty good, kind of like chicken. Needless to say he spilled the beans as to who taught him that one, and I got another phone call."

Like all families, we were five individuals with five distinct personalities. If you saw our children together, you would never know they were related because they didn't look like one another. It's remarkable—miraculous, really—how every person in the world is one-of-a-kind with different features and different fingerprints, all designed by a remarkable Creator!

Kathleen and Quinn built their own lives, getting married and blessing us with wonderful grandchildren. Kathleen was married and out of the house when she came over one day to visit me. I believe, as adults, Kathleen and Tim were a source of irritation to one another. Tim gave her a hard time, and Kathleen obliged him by losing patience. He knew what buttons to push to get a rise in her.

During this short visit she had heard Tim ask me the same question, again and again, at least a dozen times. Having been away long enough to forget how different it was living with a brother who was challenging, I'll never forget her parting remark. When she was ready to leave she said, "Mom, how can you stand it?"

I've heard how this kind of reaction is quite common. When a sibling is once out of the house the normalcy they were used to as they were growing up is no longer a part of their everyday life. They adjust to their own "normal," and it's a big change from what is typical for their mom and dad. So life goes on. And with it comes a whole new series of circumstances, experiences, and relationships. They grow into their own world—making decisions and unfortunately also making mistakes. And so it is with all of us. That's life.

> NATALIE STEWART (granddaughter): Some funny things that my Uncle Tim would do was, he'd usually give my mom a hard time. She'd tell him not to do something, but when she'd leave the room, he'd look at me and then do exactly what she told him not to do. We'd both smile and enjoy the joke on her.

People Who Cared

Tim did remarkably well and enjoyed the independence of being by himself. It was fortunate for us that he could safely stay at home alone for many hours. Tim coined the title for anyone who did stay with him as a "Tim-sitter."

I remember the day when I felt desperate about finding someone trustworthy to stay with him. This too is a problem when it comes to the disabled. The family needs to find competent, caring people, and through the years we have been very fortunate in having just that.

Patsy Layton worked for Steitz's Resort on Lake Marie, in Antioch, and we had talked to her many times when she waited on our table. John and Jan Steitz were the resort owners and close friends of ours. When Jan told me Patsy wasn't working there anymore, it gave us the opportunity to ask her about sitting with Tim.

Blessed with a happy personality and positive attitude, Patsy, a few years younger than I, became the ideal Tim-sitter. Not being married, she was readily available when we needed her, and she became one of the many golden treasures that flowed into Tim's life. Patsy loved the Cubs and enjoyed talking as much as Tim did. They were great for each other, and a close friendship developed among all of us. Tim was privileged to have many enjoyable years with this loving, caring woman—a very precious Tim-sitter.

Before Patsy, an older woman named Edythe would have Tim in her home. She'd take him out to lunch and do fun things along with watching the Cubs games with him. Their time together never ended without humorous stories being shared. We could always count on chuckles and smiles when we'd pick him up.

The ability to dial a phone by touching a button enabled Tim to contact those who cared about him. Because he was not able to dial a number, I devised a simple system that worked. He had a wall phone in his room and important phone numbers were programmed in. I painted the access buttons different colors and tacked small photos of programmed family members on the base of the phone. Each picture had a colored dot on it to correspond with that same color on the access button.

If Tim needed Pat in his office, he'd push the top button, then blue for Kathleen and Mark, red for Quinn and Kelly, and yellow for Grandma Helen Minahan, known as Gee Gee. And when we would go out at night we'd program the very last button to the place where he could get us. Tim took advantage of this convenience. If he got lonely he'd just push a button.

"And what is the meaning of this?" Tim, the wise old owl, met us as the door one night when we arrived home later than we said we'd be. Well, why not? We said we'd be home at a particular time, and as far as Tim was concerned that time was set in stone.

The Past and the Future

Gee Gee had personal insight on why Tim would worry about us. Occasionally when Mom would stay with Tim, they'd talk for all the hours we were gone. Reminiscing was a favorite pastime. Because of Tim's phenomenal memory he loved talking about things that involved him and his childhood. As the night wore on he'd begin pacing and asking whether she thought we would get home on time. If we were late he'd really be upset.

My mother figured Tim knew how much he needed us. If something were to happen to his parents, then what? As I listened to Mom it made perfect sense. It was intelligent and logical thinking on Tim's part. What would happen to him?

We could always depend on our kids to take care of Tim. Pat and I were able to take short trips or get away for a day. Kathleen and her husband, Mark, and Quinn and his wife, Kelly, would take care of all Tim's needs. This meant washing his feet, putting on his socks and shoes, shaving him, helping him on and off the toilet and up and down stairs.

Mark and Kelly had become more than just family to Tim. They became friends along with being brother—and sister-in-law. We are grateful the Lord put the perfect spouses in the lives of our children. They have been tremendous blessings to all of us, and we love them as our own.

Tim was a groomsman for Kathleen and Mark, and for Quinn and Kelly when they got married. We look at our photos with joy, knowing he was involved in all family events that meant so much. Then when Kathleen and Mark's first daughter, Amanda, was born, Tim was godfather and my niece Shawn was godmother.

There were times when we would be asked the question we dreaded the most. "Why am I this way?" "Why did God make me this way?" It wasn't easy to give an answer. But I would explain as best I could that everyone has a weakness of some kind . . . how God has a plan for each one of us, and that his particular problems just required more assistance.

> KELLY (MACK) STAGG (daughter-in-law): Tim once asked me, while taking a stroll with one of my children, "Kelly, do you think if I didn't have my problems I would have made a good dad?" And my honest answer was always the same, "The best Tim—the best."
>
> Tim was a wonderful uncle regardless of a season of life that allowed him only small, slow steps. Yet he taught four of his nieces how to walk during their toddler years. Actually, he was the perfect candidate. Tim held their hands and taught them through his love and

patience. Now as I look at two more babies, Patrick and Brandi, who were born since Tim passed, I regret he is not here to teach them to walk. But I am still thankful, because I've come to realize how this young man (some would define as crippled) taught a lot of us how to walk spiritually.

Tim knew he would have to be cared for by someone if we were no longer here for him. Both Kathleen and Quinn assured us time and again that Tim would never be put into any other home but one of theirs. Knowing how this might some day become reality, in their minds it was already done. Tim would live with them. However, we as parents made it clear we did not expect them to have this obligation, especially with children of their own. No one knows what the future holds for any of us. But with that said, our kids made it very clear: Tim's future without us would be secure with them.

What a Swob!

Day to day Tim took care of himself and kept our house in order (whether we wanted him to or not). Everything would be where it should be. There wasn't anything out of place because he would make sure drawers and doors were closed, lights were off, shoes put away, *TV Guide* and papers in the basket, sink faucet handles facing straight up, toilet seat down, countertop free from dirty dishes, and on and on. He was expert in cleaning out the dishwasher and cleaning up after himself in the bathroom. His room was spotless—not a wrinkle in his bed.

BRITTANY STAGG (granddaughter): Whenever we spent the night at Grandma and Grandpa's we could always expect to hear the sound of the *Bozo Show* that Uncle Tim watched first thing every morning. Then we'd hear the sound of the AM radio coming from the bathroom. I don't recall the program, but he was always listening to it while he got ready for the day." [He listened to Bob Collins on WGN Chicago.]

Laremont School taught Tim to set a table, and this he did faithfully for us every day. And heaven forbid if we happened to set the table and put a fork on the wrong side or a napkin askew. He'd show how disgusted he was with our ineptness as he put things right. After the grumbling we would receive a lecture.

Pat's nickname, via Tim, came to be used at least once a day. "Dad, you're sush a swob." I didn't know exactly how much that nickname fit until it was I who was putting those shoes away and turning off the lights and closing cabinets and drawers (and putting down the toilet seat). His admonishment of his father was always followed with the Timism, "This place is a real pig stile."

BRITTANY: One of my favorite memories is about the *TV Guide*. It would be around mid-afternoon when Uncle Tim would round up the usual suspects and question us on the whereabouts of the *TV Guide*. I don't ever remember actually taking it or even moving it, but this was very important to him and he had to make sure. Maybe it was his way of warning us to keep our hands off.

Tim was never at a loss for words and usually said what he thought. Many times our family would shudder at something he would say. It was usually in the company of other people, and we could pretty well be assured it was going to happen. It would come out of the blue with no warning; we became accustomed to being embarrassed.

One of those occasions took place while camping at Blackhawk Ridge. An old black Labrador named Sue was spread out on the ground resting, and Tim and I happened to be standing next to her. As a group of people passed by, old Sue did what dogs do best—with a very loud blast for added effect. Tim got this funny look on his face. As his eyes widened big as saucers he turned to me and bellowed for all to hear, "Was that you, Mom?"

Pat, Tim, and I were having dinner at a widowed aunt's home along with her male friend, a widower, who recently moved into Aunt May's apartment with her. (Names changed to protect the innocent!) As the five of us were enjoying our meal, Tim did it again. He asked Aunt May where George slept. Tim knew there was only one bedroom, and after thinking about this, it got the best of him. Without forewarning—"zap"—out it came.

We all sat motionless knowing the only one who could answer the question was Aunt May. After a few seconds she told him that George slept in the bedroom. Well, that answer did not satisfy Tim's curiosity—or was it a test? Now he pressed. "Yes . . . but, where does he sleep?" Poor Aunt May could do nothing but say, "He sleeps in the bed." Tim also knew there was only one bed. That was the end of test!

Sometimes if I struggled to find a solution to a problem, Tim and I would talk about it and many times he'd come up with the perfect commonsense answer. Other times he'd put in his two cents and we'd laugh at his off-the-wall advice. If I asked his opinion on something I was wearing, I knew he would give me the right dope. "It makes you look fat." And he was right.

One day I asked if he liked my new orange-red suit with the matching plaid blouse. "No, you look like you're going trick-or-treating." I realize I cannot wear that color and probably resembled a clown. Tim was gifted with common sense in a way from which we all could take lessons.

After he heard a warning about hair coloring on the news, he gave us the report. "They're warning ladies not to have their gray show, it's dangerous for their head." I'll never remember the hundreds of cute sayings we heard, but if I could repeat them they would surely fill a book all by themselves. Like the time he asked, "If you sneeze all the time, will your nose get bigger?" But the one I really love is a Timism he used to describe a new grandchild born into the family. It was December 1992, and his comment: "A bungle of joy."

One Sunday afternoon we had a family get-together at our home. Pat came from a family of seven children so we could always count on a pretty good crowd. Everyone was having a great time, and as the day progressed, we wondered what had happened to my brother-in-law.

Pat's sister Diane and her husband Harold did come together, but later in the day Harold could not be found—he just disappeared. It wasn't until the next day that Tim told me he sent Uncle Harold home because he was spilling his drink and missing the ashtray. Quinn remembered Tim saying to him, "My mom is going to be real mad, so you better go home." And I'll bet a lecture, with hand on hip, followed Harold to the door.

Our times of laughter with Tim will forever outweigh his years of suffering and pain. Pat's mother, Grandma Sue, who was now in her late 70s, sat in our kitchen complaining about how old she was getting. Tim followed up with, "Ah Grandma, don't feel so bad, you're not as old as you look." My ears still ring with the howling that followed. One day the kids were giving Pat a hard time because his hair was turning gray. Tim put his arm around Pat's shoulders, "Don't feel bad, Dad, you look very extinguished with gray hair."

I was feeling especially good one morning after being sick for a couple of weeks and it must have surprised Tim. As I continued goofing around and acting silly with him, he finally questioned, "Are you drunk, Mom?" When I answered, "Certainly not!" he asked, "Well, did you have too much breakfast?"

Because Tim used a cane, he acquired an assortment of canes from all over the country. Friends and relatives would pick one up for him in their travels. There are twenty-seven standing like sentinels in the entrance hall to our home. They fit into an old metal Boy Scout water container I bought in an antique shop. It's perfect, with an opening large enough for all of them and room to spare. My friend Eileen

Ostrander gave us an article on the history of canes that was so interesting I put it in clear plastic, attached a ribbon to it and hung it there for all to read.

Abnormal Endurance

Tim had pain in different parts of his body every day of his life, and when he'd complain he'd say, "My poor knees," or "My poor back," or "My poor" whatever. I guess we used this term too without even realizing it. In the back of our minds we just thought, "Our poor Tim."

If mornings are dull for most folks, they sure weren't for us. Before we were out of bed Tim could be heard humming a variety of great tunes. He was still in bed, and it was like the birds you hear chirping before your eyes are open. He had an ear for music and memorized songs. So before we could focus and see what kind of day it was, we would hear him chirping and it would put a smile on our faces.

Tim was exact about everything and very independent. He wouldn't let anyone do anything for him that he could do himself, and he'd get a 10-plus for cleanliness. If we were sick we'd get a lecture about keeping our hands clean and taking our vitamins like he did. We could always count on a pointed finger aiming directly at one of us with the statement, "Don't you want to die healthy?"

The funny, unexpected comments that came out of Tim continue to fill our lives with the same laughter as when they were first spoken. If there was tension or times of heated words, Tim could defuse the situation in a heartbeat. However, there were times when he was the cause of the tension and we would have to use "tough love." He wasn't a saint by a long shot, but he was a genuinely good, decent person.

> KELLY: I thought about how much my life was touched by knowing my brother-in-law Tim. I realize there are many things I could write about, like his uncanny memory for detail, his laugh, his jokes, and his smile. He loved children and life itself, and he loved God. But my most obvious memory is the images of him I will always have—a man who often taught me something important whether he knew it or not.

One morning Tim said, "I have to go outside now," and I answered, "Well, not until you give me a hug." After his, "Okay," he hung his cane on the bathroom towel hook, came over and put his arm around me. He snuggled his face into my neck and then gave me a kiss. Before leaving he said, "Only one thing left, I'm sorry for this morning." "That's okay, Tim, it happens to all of us. We all say things at times when we don't mean it." "Why, Mom?" he questioned. "Well, that's just being human, Tim." (Oh, for just one more hug!)

Many times he and I would tell each other how really sorry we were for being impatient, or speaking harshly, or for some other reason. And anytime he needed to make amends he'd draw a self-portrait of himself as a peace offering. He'd also present one as a gift for just about any occasion. Each time I find one a little jolt inside me rises up into a smile. These precious drawings appear in drawers and boxes; tucked between pages of books and albums; and rest in just about every nook and cranny of our old house.

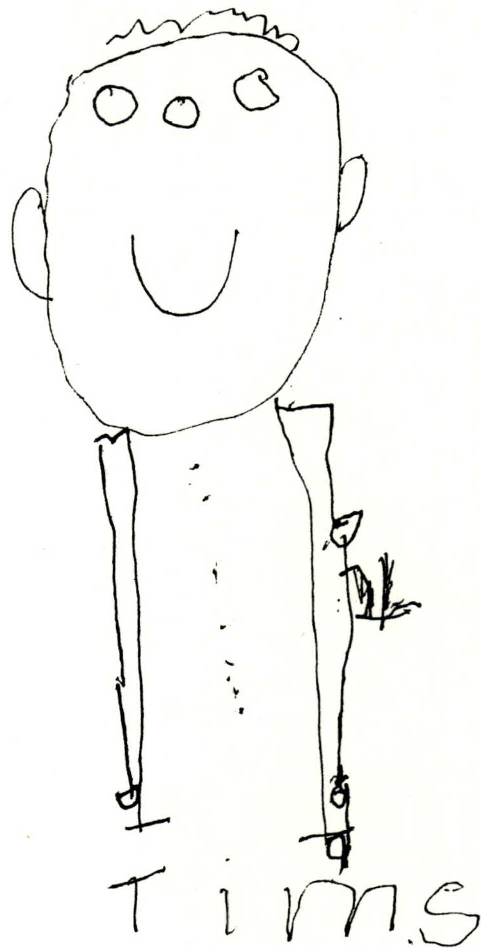

One of Tim's self-portraits (with a cane)

For several years we had a pontoon boat that was easy to get on and off of along with comfortable seats for Tim. One day Gayle Ranker joined us for a cruise, and she brought her friend Joan along. It was our normal day, full of fun and laughter, and when Joan left for home she couldn't thank us enough.

A week later Tim received a package in the mail. It was a prized baseball signed by Babe Ruth and Lou Gehrig. Joan had asked her grown children if they would mind if she gave the ball to him, and they said it would be okay. Giving up that cherished baseball was just another gesture of love from someone (like so many) who had been touched by Tim.

Tim's sunshine world—a blend of innocence and wisdom—was infectious. Even a short visit into his realm would challenge you to wonder. . . . For example, if you don't think you can believe in Santa Claus no matter how old you are, you'd better think again. Tim was thirty-eight and a true believer in that jolly old elf. Nothing we said or did would convince him otherwise. He knew Jesus Christ as his Lord and Savior. But Santa, well, he was not someone he was willing to let go of. He had a clear vision of who God was and who Santa was.

When I told this to my sister Sharon, she replied with a lilt to her voice assuring me she too still believes in Santa. See what I mean? With St. Nicholas being a real person and a great deal having been written about him down through history, I can hear Tim say, "Case closed!"

That also brings to mind Tim's reasoning when it came to the folks who give the weather report each day. Unfortunately for them, our weathermen and women, he showed no mercy. In his mind they were the cause of all bad weather. If you report the weather—you'd better be able to do something about it!

Grandma Sue Stagg and the dancin' machine

With that jolly old elf

Watching over Amanda, Natalie, & Brittany

Kathleen's wedding, May 1980

A young Mark and Tim

Patsy, Gee Gee, & Edythe at Tim's surprise birthday party

CHAPTER 6

The Security of School

Prom week, seventeen-year-old Tim said: "Mom, I'm telling you, I'm going to knock everyone's socks off. Yes, really, wait and see. I'll knock 'em loose with a new technique. I'm going to do my fancy footwork."

Laremont School, SEDOL's permanent facility, was built in a spacious country setting in Gages Lake, Illinois. Laremont was named after Larry Vuilmont, the first superintendent. It was a Cadillac in design and equipped and built for very special people with all their needs in mind, including a heated pool for therapy.

Best of all were the superior teachers and therapists who worked with the kids to bring out every ounce of untapped ability per individual. Our children were in good hands and we knew it; parents had assurance the best was being given them.

Because of the large number of people we are indebted to, I will not mention names. But this book is also a tribute, with thanks, to the diligent people so devoted to their profession with the disabled. Teachers, therapists, social workers, aides, administrators, and everyone involved, along with bus drivers who took our kids to and from school safely . . . they all played a big part in Tim's life.

Tim loved school and had a close bond of friendship with his classmates and his teachers. He learned how to take care of his personal needs with in-depth training in a way I would not have been able to do. With Tim not being able to bend his knees, he could not put on his shoes or socks. So a special stick designed in physical therapy enabled him to put on his pants and under shorts, and take them off along with his socks and even his shoes. It didn't take long for him to become proficient with it, which made life for him and us a little easier.

Casey Sinkledam was the head chef at Kitchens of Sara Lee and coworker of our friend Gayle Ranker. He met Tim the day of the MDA picnic when Tim and Jerry Lewis put on their lively performance, and it was his large clown cake that was served.

Casey was famous for creating life-size portraits made entirely of frosting. He wanted to do something special for Tim, so he designed a clown picture out of frosting and presented it to Laremont School in Tim's honor. And thinking back on all of this, it's amazing to me how Tim found himself in the presence of some very important people, again and again.

We were told Casey's artistic creations hung in many places across the country. When Pat and I were in Galena, Illinois, we saw one of his portraits, encased in glass, hanging in the old railroad station now used as an information center.

We Learn with Experience

Tim grew and matured into a wonderful young man. He graduated when he was twenty-one, and he was able to say that he truly enjoyed school. Memories of those precious years would be numerous, including the great prom nights sponsored by Kemper Insurance in Long Grove. The backdrop was their beautifully landscaped acreage. Driving up to the building complex where the prom was held was very impressive for these special kids. Kemper provided the flowers, the dinner, and the music for dancing.

The 1980 graduating class from Laremont School presented the Kemper Group with a plaque in appreciation of their hosting the annual school prom since 1972. Tim and his good friend Carlos Cabal were chosen to be the ones to give the award to Kemper's Community Relations Coordinator, Carol Lood. And a photo of the presentation, with Tim grinning from ear to ear, was in our local newspaper.

I received a phone call shortly before prom that year. Tim's teacher wanted to know if he would be at the dance because he was picked to be Laremont's prom king. Joan Strum, one of Tim's best friends, was chosen to be their queen. Our pictures reveal how surprised and proud Tim was to be given such an honor. Joan had cerebral palsy and needed a wheelchair. But this didn't keep her off the dance floor with those around her moving her wheels to the music. Nothing was held back for these wonderful young men and women.

Homecoming dances after graduation came around every October, the perfect place to renew friendships. There were handshakes and hugs and a night full of music and fun. Then it was over too quickly and another year would pass before the excitement of meeting old chums would well up once again.

Graduation was getting close, and Laremont planned a visit to a sheltered workshop twenty miles from our home. Workshops for handicapped adults are similar to a school environment. They provide work on easy projects and the opportunity to socialize with friends. Wages are minimal, but the working aspect and interaction with others is good therapy.

Those who cannot concentrate on counting, sorting, or packing can instead spend their days participating in social activities. Workshops also afford parents the opportunity to have a more normal life and at the same time give their adult children a feeling of independence.

Parents were invited to tour one of these facilities along with Tim's graduating class, so Pat and I joined them. This particular workshop provided a program for the mentally disabled as well as the emotionally and mentally ill.

There is a vast difference between mental retardation and mental illness. For the most part, those who Tim went to school with were gentle, loving, likable kids. They had been well trained at Laremont, and they cared about one another. Laremont provided a safe, healthy place for them every day.

As we toured the building, Pat and I walked through rows of kids who were sitting and standing at their workstations. They looked happy, and we recognized some as former graduates of Laremont. All of a sudden a large man became extremely agitated and lifted a chair above his head. As he was about to fling it across the room, attendants were able to stop him.

This was upsetting for us to see, but we felt it happened for a reason. As we continued making our way through the rows and rooms of workers, I was becoming concerned for their safety. I managed to ask one or two if they liked being there and their answer was "Yes." But they, with their innocence, could not recognize the fact that they were among a few people who could lose control and someone could get hurt—maybe not intentionally, but nonetheless they were in a risky place. At least that was the impression both Pat and I had. To be fair, I'm sure many other parents would not agree with us, but they didn't see what we did.

The tour ended, and as we walked through a hallway toward the front door, we looked into the room where they had taken the man who was going to throw the chair. He was on the floor and an assistant was sitting on him, I suppose, until he calmed down. Reactions to situations can be altogether different from a person who is mentally ill over the one who is mentally retarded. No, this was not the place for Tim.

"Let's not say anything to Tim about the workshop, and let him tell us how he feels about it first." I threw this out to Pat and he agreed. When Tim's bus dropped him off, I met him at the door. He was probably thinking about that place all afternoon because his foot wasn't over the threshold when I heard, "I don't want to go to that workshop, Mom." This was another logical, intelligent reaction to something that would affect him, and we were happy he could see the difference. We assured him he'd never have to go there.

How facilities are funded makes a difference. Most sheltered programs keep the mentally disabled separated from those with emotional and mental problems. A couple of workshops we knew of provided excellent programs that would have been very good for Tim, but they did not have bus service to our rural area.

Tough Testing—Simple Solution

Before graduation, Laremont students were tested at the Lake County Area Vocational Center in a testing program designed for SEDOL. The simulated workshops gave the staff an idea on how successful their efforts were in training students for jobs out in the community. A large number of businesses and institutions employ graduates who attended special education. These kids have proven to be trustworthy, diligent, hard workers. The testing program called Vocational Assessment covered various areas to determine interest and worker traits with each graduate.

We met with the team who tested Tim, and Pat and I could feel the frustration coming through as they began to explain their assessment. They would like to have given us a good report, but their disappointment showed. In every area of testing Tim scored zero. The final report reads: Tim a twenty-year-old student, attempted each task in a positive manner but became frustrated and confused after working for a short period of time. When asked if he understood the directions after they were given, he would reply, "Yes."

After administering tests in which Tim showed an interest, such as food service, clerical, and patient care, the following conclusion was given: In view of Tim's physical limitations and his mental capabilities the Assessment Lab does not possess the adequate tasks to evaluate his skills. Pat and I understood this concluding statement as a delicate way of telling parents their child could not be evaluated.

Having thought through the situation before meeting with the team, we were already prepared. I guess we knew Tim would not pass the testing. We were considering an area that had not been thought of before, and we were ready to suggest it. "Could Tim volunteer in a nursing home during their social time? He has great skills interacting with the elderly, and we know he could do it. He walks with a cane and he'd fit right in." The staff had never considered Laremont students as volunteering in a nursing home. After a moment of reflection they liked the idea and then became very enthusiastic.

The wheels were put into motion, and the day arrived when Tim would have an interview with director of Hillcrest Nursing Center. His teacher who prepared him for this interview could see he was visibly nervous. Once again, a logical reaction on Tim's part led him to realize that this was a very important step for him. As questions were asked, Tim answered each one correctly until, "Do you have any brothers or sisters?" In his nervous state he answered, "No." But anyone who knew Tim knew he loved talking about Kathleen and Quinn and his family. He got the job!

Giving a Little of Himself

Tim was faithful in his commitment that began during his last year of school and continued for two years after graduation. The same bus that picked Tim up each day for school dropped him off at Hillcrest in the early afternoon for two hours, two days a week. After graduation he went three days a week, and the community bus called PACE picked him up at our door. It had a lift like a school bus and made it easy for Tim to get on and off.

As far as we knew he mixed well with the residents of Hillcrest who met in the social room and cafeteria. The original director knew all about Tim's habits, strengths, and weaknesses—what he could and could not do. And if there was ever a problem they were to call us.

Quite a span of time had passed when I decided to call Hillcrest to see how Tim was doing. A new social director had been hired, and it was apparent she didn't realize his limitations. Nor did she know she should have called us. She was very kind and sort of hesitant as she let me know, "There are a few problems."

I was disappointed to hear this and needed to know every detail. She explained several things. "First, when Tim comes into the building he goes straight to the TV and turns on the station he wants when everyone is watching something else." (I bet he turned on the Cubs.) "Second, when Tim is told to go to room such and such to see if the lights were off, he refuses to go." The TV problem I assured her would be taken care of right away. Once Tim was told I knew it would not happen again. The other problem was something else.

Tim did not know right from left. Nor would he be able to find any specific room by number. But I do know he was required at times to walk the halls and tell people who had lights on, to please turn them off. He was faithful in the things he could do. Once it was planted in his head it was there forever.

I can't recall the third problem, but by now the poor lady felt pretty bad. After discussing all the things he couldn't do, her kind response was, "Well, he does really well when he plays checkers with the patients."

With that, I just replied with a hearty chuckle, "Tim can't play checkers." Can you put yourself in this woman's shoes? How frustrating! But now she had a little more insight and understanding on just who this nervy, unwilling kid with the cane was. I'm sure things became less stressful for both Tim and those who oversaw activities.

As months came and went, Tim was getting sick more often. It was obvious the elderly residents, being confined indoors, were continually passing their germs on to one another. I made up my mind if Tim came down with another cold we wouldn't let him go back. So with that, it wasn't long before Tim was again very sick. The scoliosis of his upper back was crowding his lungs, making it difficult for him to cough hard enough to clear his lungs. Any cold or virus became dangerous. Before I had a chance to say anything, Tim announced, "I don't think I should go back to Hillcrest anymore. Everyone's sick."

Tim's adventures at the nursing home ended. It had been a very positive experience that broadened his education. Pat and I always gained from whatever Tim was involved in, and the nursing home was no different. Along with his hilariously funny stories, it gave us awareness on how the people there reacted to him and to one another. On April 19, 1983, he received a certificate: *In Grateful Appreciation to Tim Stagg for Volunteer Services in the Social Program of Hillcrest Retirement Village, Inc.*

Several years later when Grandma Sue Stagg was a resident at Hillcrest, Tim and I went to see her. A sweet woman who lived there for a long time remembered Tim from his volunteer days. She was thrilled and excited to see him and told me how she would never forget the wonderful and kind way he had always treated her. I was happy to see Tim had befriended someone who didn't have family close by, as she was probably the only Afro-American patient living there at that time. Tim was her friend and she missed him. Many aids and workers were also friendly and kind to Tim and went out of their way to talk to him whenever we ran into them.

Now as we reflect on the many years that have passed and the many people who crossed Tim's path, the Lord used him in ways that we can't begin to imagine. Only when we see him again in the presence of Jesus will we know how many were blessed by his touch.

> KELLY: First of all I praise God that He created Tim, and with delight, in His own image. Now most people wouldn't see it that way. How can a man who was so defined by physical limitations appear to be created in the image of a God of perfection? But he was, and through this creation mystery, Tim's life continually revealed God's glory. Not only to me, but to the many lives he touched.

Special Olympics

School provided the opportunity for another door to be opened to the handicapped: Special Olympics. It was a thrill for us to experience this great event right along with the kids. Tim participated in wheelchair races—winning some, losing some, but always collecting a blue, red, or white ribbon that went with it. He also participated in a swimming competition at Buffalo Grove High School, swimming the backstroke in an Olympic-size pool. It was something to see as he followed directions from the instructor to the finish.

One day in particular stands out in our minds. Pat and I remember with a smile the little guy with Down syndrome who ran a race well ahead of all the others. As the roar of the crowd and their clapping reached his ears, it was too much for him to ignore. He couldn't resist. He stopped, smiled from ear to ear, turned toward the cheering crowd with both arms raised high in triumph as the rest of the runners ran past him to the finish line.

Even though this enthusiastic racer wasn't first at the finish line he did not lose. In the Special Olympics there are no losers. Special? Yes. They are all special, and we should not have a world without them. And, I believe, that is exactly what God had in mind. Each special child runs a race unlike anything you or I can relate to. It begins at birth and ends with God as He presents them with their prize of distinction. It is given to REAL WORLD-CLASS PARTICIPANTS. And the prize they receive is a heavenly one—a prize only given to special people.

Tim's school experiences were positive and exciting. His brain's ability to journal made up for not being able to read or write. Like a camera that never stops, his mind was soaking up everything he saw and heard. That imperfect brain, which was so different, could store and record way beyond what we would consider normal.

Tim could recall situations from long ago, what someone wore, what color it was, or where something took place, as if it were yesterday. If you had new glasses and he hadn't seen you in a year he would let you know how nice your new glasses were. It was Halloween of '85 and he remembered Grandma Stagg had been in the hospital at that time the year before. He could recognize places and locations even though it would have been a long time since being there. Yes, he had a remarkable mind, and he used it to the fullest.

The word Halloween has jogged my memory in the way Tim explained it to us one year. "Today the cats and rats and witches and bats meet." I asked who told him that and he replied, "Oh, I don't know, I probably made it up." For sure he made it up.

We think Tim's descriptions of people and situations, at times, were far more interesting and a great deal more fun to listen to. He returned from the October '92 Homecoming dance and told us that a teacher called classmates Norman Glowacki and his brother, "Long legged daddy legs." Because they were so tall, we figured he meant "Daddy long legs." If smiling and laughter is good for the soul, the Lord surely blessed our lives with smiles in abundance.

Good friend Tim Mahoney

Our three teenagers

Wheelchair race for Special Olympics

Won a red ribbon

Proud to be Prom King

Graduation Day, 1981

CHAPTER 7

An Innovative Mind

Tim asked, "Where did I come from Dad?" Pat answered, "God sent you to us." . . . Tim: "Oh yes, I remember. God asked me, 'Are you ready Tim?'" With the knowledge of how God had His hand on Tim, I ponder over those words—and I wonder.

I called Tim "Mr. Belvedere" after that meticulous and lovable TV character, because he was so particular about himself and the limited world around him, our home. In spite of what he was capable of doing he needed constant reminders. He'd stay in the bathroom combing his hair until lunchtime if we let him. When we weren't around, he didn't have to hurry and loved it that way. Most of the time he would hear us pleading, "Will you please get out of there?"

One birthday Tim got an electric razor, but he used it until his face become red and sore. Because he could not shave himself with a regular razor I took over the job. This turned out to be an ongoing blessing, as it became one of the most enjoyable times we spent together. It was close and loving, and the Lord used it as a spiritual remembrance the day Tim died.

Sometimes grocery shopping was put off until we were desperate. One morning our cupboards were bare, and as I rushed out the door I yelled to Tim that I'd be home soon with lots of food. He was capable of making cold cereal and toast, pouring juice, and making a cup of tea with an electric teakettle. He never had to touch the stove. It would have been dangerous if he did. But this particular day for some reason, he decided to do something different.

Tim couldn't stand a guilty conscience and usually came clean about anything that worried him. So when I returned, it was only a few minutes when he told me, "I got an egg out of the refrigerator and was going to cook it, but I wasn't able to because it dropped on the floor." I was surprised to hear him say he was going to cook. I looked for egg on my white kitchen floor and began to doubt it was true. It could be his way of making a point to let me know he couldn't find anything to eat.

Looking again I still couldn't find a trace of egg. Then he said, "I cleaned it up." With that, I got on my hands and knees and to my amazement found a minute speck of yellow. "How on earth did you clean it up?" Tim's unbelievable answer, "I used my cane and a dish cloth." Impossible! There's no way! I could never clean up a broken egg, shell and all, with a cane and dishcloth. Try it sometime.

I know without a doubt God protected Tim over and over again. This time the egg dropped, preventing him from turning on the stove. The slippery egg could cause him to fall if he stepped or put his cane in it. This situation is added to all the times when God's power was evident. I don't question for a moment that the Lord's protection surrounded him. And in all my journaling, after each entry such as this is written, "Thank You Lord!"

Day of Disclosure

"You worry things too much," or "Your imagination is going around with you" were statements directed to me that I heard often. But the one Tim used the most was, "You watch me like a hawk." He really couldn't do too much that we didn't know about, and it was for his benefit that we did. So it was with surprise that I discovered a side of him I didn't know—Mr. Neatnik was about to be exposed.

Tim's bedroom held most of his possessions. He had his TV and VCR, boom box, radio, shortwave, CDs, tapes (especially the Beach Boys), and his special chair. Rearranging furniture in this crowded room was seldom done. But this day Tim could see I was about to move the dresser and hutch as I began taking off books and keepsakes. In a quiet tone he muttered, "Oh, oh, are you in for a big surprise," and hightailed it out of the room.

His statement didn't mean anything until I started the slow process of moving the dresser away from the wall. Immediately my eyes caught sight of an array of brightly colored wrappers. They were from candy, gum, and stuff he had consumed in probably two years. The dresser was up against a built-in bunk bed with a solid base, the perfect place for quick disposal of unwanted garbage.

From Mr. Neatnik to what . . . I can't call him a litterbug because he didn't litter. The "wrapper trasher" is more like it. This bit of newsy gossip spread throughout our family like wildfire and was received with disbelief. Everyone knew what a perfectionist Tim was. This was delightful news and I couldn't resist saving it on film. If you can, picture colored wrappers stuffed in a crowded corner with the more recent ones clinging to the wall with nowhere else to go but up. I put the whole hodgepodge collection in a large, clear plastic bag for all to see. And with this permanent display, one with an imaginative mind might think of it as an ingenious piece of creative artwork.

The brightly colored candy & gum wrappers

The Ultimate Messenger

Quinn had a job working nights stocking shelves for a local grocery chain. On days off his boss would call and ask him to come in. Now, Quinn didn't want to work on his day off, but couldn't get up the nerve to say no and would grudgingly go in. "Tell the truth, Quinn," I told him. "Just tell your boss you don't want to work on your day off."

On one such day, Quinn nervously awaited that dreaded call. I wasn't home so he told Tim if the phone rang and it was his boss, "Tell him I'm not home." Sure enough the phone rang and it was his boss. From the living room Quinn could hear those wonderful words, "No, Quinn's not at home." Then the neatest thing happened. His boss asked when Quinn would be home. Without hesitation, Tim walked to the doorway with phone in hand and called out, "Hey Quinn, he wants to know when you'll be home?" Putting the phone back up to his ear Tim replied, "He said he'll be home later."

Quinn never lived this one down, and Tim—well—what more can be said? Two thumbs up! Quinn's boss never said anything, and I don't think he ever called him again on a day off.

Sometimes Tim would answer the phone, and it was obvious he was talking to someone from school or camp. One evening he had a call, but after awhile he sounded confused. I asked who it was and he couldn't tell me. When I took the phone, the voice on the other end was a Marine recruiting officer calling for Tim Stagg. And of course he knew he had been talking to Tim Stagg.

Quickly I apologized and briefly explained why Tim was not eligible for military service. I really don't know if he believed me. The way Tim would have answered questions might sound more like someone trying to get out of something. I envision the recruiter scratching his head, possibly cussin' in God's veins.

My cousin Frank Prokop, an ex-Marine, was also Tim's godfather. It was ironic how the symbol of the Marines was an influence that touched Tim's life through Frank. He had given Tim so many nice things through the years, including shirts, hats, and other items with the Marine insignia. Frank explained it as a tribute to the brave and honorable way Tim endured all the battles he experienced, both physically and mentally. And in the very end, appropriately, Tim received a Marine medal.

Common Sense Works

Tim had more surgeries than we want to remember. Many did not relate to his everyday problems but for things like a hernia and gallbladder removal. Often, Pat and I would be ready to leave for the hospital to visit or to bring him home when our phone would ring. Soon we'd anticipate that ring, and sure enough it would be Tim. He'd ask a nurse or dial the operator himself and explain in his halting speech that he was handicapped and not able to dial a number, and the operator would take time to listen. Without fail, he was connected to the most important thing in his life—his home and his parents.

Our niece Shawn had an emergency with her baby, Molly, so I dropped everything and drove her to Children's Memorial in Chicago. I left so fast Tim knew it was serious. When we arrived at Children's, the nurse said my son had called and I was sure it must have been Quinn. Then immediately another call came in for me and it was Tim. He dialed a regular operator telling her he needed Children's Memorial, and when he got the hospital he gave the name of Molly Brennan. The hospital operator plugged him into the right floor and desk.

One day I was about to call a relative person to person and Tim asked, "Are you going to make a head-to-head call?" Tim's keen observations came through daily experiences, and he used the knowledge he acquired to manage all areas of his life. With what you are about to read, I will repeat, all areas of his life. You can be the judge!

> MARK: About two years before Tim went to be with our Lord, he stayed with us for a few days while his mom and dad were away. It was fun having him here, but it kind of messed up his usual routine not being at home. Sunday morning Kath and our girls went to church. I told them Tim and I would stay home and watch the Three Stooges, you know, guy stuff.
>
> Well, after breakfast and a little TV, Tim needed to use the bathroom. He wasn't really very agile, so you needed to help him on and off the porcelain throne. After awhile he called to me that he was ready to get up, so I went in the bathroom, turned the exhaust fan on super high, and started giving him heck about the funny smell. Well, I didn't know the routine at home, and

again, Tim couldn't move very well. So I asked him if he wiped himself or if his mom usually helped him. He thought for a second, then looked at me and said, "You better do it."

Now I don't know about you, but I didn't have a technique for wiping somebody else's butt other than my own. If you can picture a whole roll of toilet paper wrapped around a person's arm from the tips of his fingers up to the elbow then you pretty much captured my new technique. Tim seemed pretty serious the whole time, so I figured that was standard procedure.

A couple of days later my wife, after talking to Raquel, laughed hysterically as she informed me that the above was not standard procedure. Tim always took care of his bathroom needs by himself. I'd been had—I think. So don't be fooled about Mr. Innocent. He had his ways to get back when he wanted to.

Prayer Partner

Prayers were interwoven into Tim's life. We believe they are the keys that open doors here on earth and doors into heavenly places. Prayers were part of our tucking-in time as Tim and I ended our day. One night he prayed for three astronauts who were preparing for their trip to the moon. He ended by announcing, "And I'll sing the Star-Spangled Banner if you want."

After a tragic school bus accident he remarked, "Life is so dainty" (meaning delicate). His genuine concern for those with disabilities, or for the sick and suffering, was real. He prayed long prayers for them and for those in the armed services who couldn't be home with their families. Sometimes his prayers went on so long I had to ask him to please stop so I could go to bed.

> MARK: Well, obviously you can tell I had a lot of fun with Tim, but there was also a very serious and compassionate side to him. Time and time again, Tim would try to cheer up others and was very sincere and heartfelt for their well-being. He never complained once to me about his physical handicaps or leaning disabilities—or just the hardships of "his world," his everyday struggles. I think of how often I complain about the smallest things and not once heard Tim complain. But in my eyes, he had every right to. I owe a lot to Tim for opening my eyes to how blessed I am and to remember there is always somebody out there worse off.

Mornings began with a rigid routine and having breakfast together. Tim would be alone for many meals, so times we could eat together were important to him. We would eat and pray as we started our day.

Because reading and memorizing prayers was something I grew up with, praying from the heart, in my own words, was new to me. Through Bible studies I learned how to pray and how to use Scripture as prayer. It changed my life, and the lives of Pat and our children.

Before this time, however, Kathleen was only eleven when she questioned me about God because her prayers were not being answered. Even though I wasn't praying, I told her to stop praying for herself and start praying for others. She did, and to my surprise prayers were being answered. People would call with prayer needs and she'd recruit others to pray for them with her. This continued into her working years, and I witnessed the ongoing results.

Meanwhile as I continued my search for truth, I read something that stirred my spirit. It was about atheists who believe in communism but have no belief in God. They question how anyone can believe in a God who tortures, maims, and kills. I read this and knew I couldn't believe in a God like that either! At that very instant, within my heart, I realized that the God I was searching for was a loving God—a God who truly loves us. Now I needed to find out more, and my heart and mind turned to Jesus. I needed a Bible.

I concluded, people make the choice to follow a loving, merciful God. And while good people also suffer because heartaches and troubles befall everyone, God promises to carry them through the storm. That day was one of many in the process that drew me into a relationship with Him. A light had turned on. Life on earth is only a very temporary existence; there's much more to our being born than just living and dying for no reason. Really . . . think about it!

After my ten-year abandonment of prayer, I decided to pray for others too. But because God had seemed so remote to me, I told myself that if I pray again I'll pray to Jesus, something I hadn't done before. I reasoned that He walked the earth—people saw Him, talked to Him, touched Him. He became as "real" to me as he was to those who wrote about him.

My inner peace came when I accepted Jesus as my personal Lord and Savior through the study of the book of Mark in the New Testament. All the burdens I carried since my childhood were lifted. These burdens are baggage filled with worldly trappings and the guilt that goes with it . . . the weight growing heavier by the year. I was free . . . free at last!

Even though my weak human nature still gets in the way, I need only to ask for forgiveness. Once again I am forgiven—a mighty, awesome reward I don't deserve! Our spiritual growth is ongoing. It's a lifetime process, and we never stop learning. Tim's life underwent this same process of spiritual growth and maturity.

God is faithful in His promises to be with us. He is God the Father; He is Jesus, God the Son (my friend); He is God the Holy Spirit (my guide and director). He gives me strength, encouragement, discernment, and protection. Old Testament Scripture tells us in Isaiah 41:10–13: "So do not fear, for I am with you; do not be dismayed, for I am your God. I will strengthen you and help you; I will uphold you with my righteous right hand. For I am the Lord, your God who takes hold of your right hand and says to you, Do not fear; I will help you."

By Whose Standards?

Many today say truth is whatever you want to believe—that there are no absolutes. By whose standards then do they live by? I was shown spiritual truths that I did not have, and my life was changed. I was still Patti, but my heart was transformed. This becomes reality for anyone who has a sincere desire to know God. Most importantly we recognize the difference between Creator and creation, and we desire to worship the Lord and not what He created!

Tim was one of today's throwaways, and yet his life held more of what it is we are looking for as we strive for perfection. And what is perfection? The world says it is the perfect mind, the perfect body, the perfect—everything. What happens when we are no longer that perfect being? Where do our hearts turn when an accident leaves us disabled or we become ill or grow old?

My eighty-nine-year-old Aunt Anna had a keen sense about her and a mind as clear as a bell, but she was legally blind. Her blindness did not stop her from going places and doing things. She did not sit at home. And I remember how upset she was when I visited her in the hospital because she was going to miss the graduation at Great Lakes Naval Base that weekend. Why she would want to do that at any time is a mystery to me, but it opened my eyes to the fact that, as long as she was alive and well, she was going to use every moment to its fullest. The following is excerpted from a letter I sent to an uncaring doctor when my aunt needed someone to come to her aid:

> As a mother of a multiple handicapped 33-year-old son, I believe with all my heart there is a purpose in this world for the handicapped. I could write a book on how his life has touched the lives of many. What a self-centered, selfish existence life would be if the only thing we cared about is what is best for *me*. The New Age thinking prevalent today says if one cannot be productive or measure up to *their* standards, than the world would be better off without him or her. Such a mindset

is being applied this very moment to infants and the elderly in a society void of absolutes, and one where *self* is deified. The system of ethics and values is almost nonexistent.

My Aunt Anna (and everyone in her situation) needs a truly caring person to oversee his and her medical needs—someone with a heart for serving others and not just to collect a fee for stopping by. Our request today, Doctor, if you cannot be this person to my aunt, then we would like you to select a doctor who is willing to provide adequate medical care and not begrudge it. If we do not hear from you within the week, we will assume you are seeking a doctor to take your place.

I want to leave one last thought—one that we do not have to agree on, but nevertheless from my standpoint, it's very important to share with you.

In the book of John in the New Testament, chapter 9, verses 1–3, Jesus was asked why a certain young man was born blind. "Who sinned? Was it the young man or his parents?" And Jesus answered, "It was neither. It was in order that God's work might be revealed." Jesus healed the young man and God was glorified through it.

God is working in the lives of people like my son and my aunt whether one likes it or not. That we may not recognize it or understand it is not important. What is important is that God is being glorified because the lives of others are being touched.

The doctor called me. He was shocked. He never saw himself as I described him in my full letter. It explained the reality of why my aunt ended up in serious condition because of his lack of concern and proper treatment, and his lying about it. He was so moved by my letter he had difficulty speaking, and with tears, asked for forgiveness. He also asked if I would come to talk to him some time. There's no doubt in my mind a spiritual hand touched this man that day. My aunt passed away soon after.

I also know that compassion misapplied in the other direction is equally as bad as the lack of compassion. At times doctors go beyond what is ethical, creating even more problems by trying to keep a patient alive. A sense of balance needs to be exercised by the medical community in which care is given within limits. Patients need to prepare for death when it is imminent, rather than the endless attempts by others to delay it.

In some hospitals today, another extreme is practiced where babies born with Down syndrome and spina bifida, along with the slightest imperfections, are deemed unfit. They are being set aside and not given medical care or food until they are too weak to even cry for help. They simply die. *This to me is the ultimate cussin' in God's veins.*

Chuck Colson's book *How Now Shall We Live* reveals how evil we have become in order to achieve the perfect society. The stunning truth is uncovered in one large volume and shows a deeply disturbing worldview—one without name or label. The Western mind, having been sold a bill of goods, has substituted the kingdom of God for the "religion" of science and its espousing utopia. It's difficult to comprehend how we are already at the place where babies are left to die if they are not wanted. This should torment the very core of our soul.

This is not God's plan. How many times have we read about mothers who were advised to abort but went on to deliver normal, healthy babies? I personally know several of these moms.

Those wanting to rid society of the unwanted cleverly use the civilized terms, "mercy killing," "wrongful birth," and "choice." This philosophy basically teaches that some people are less valuable than others, and they are not worth the material cost. But I tell you without reservation, there will be a cost one way or another. We are going to pay a price.

No, there's much more to life. If you do not believe in a God who loves you and has a purpose for your life, then you are missing out on what life is all about. Having a relationship with God gives us hope and opens our minds to the answers everyone is frantically looking for. The problem? They are looking in all the wrong places—they need to begin with the heart.

The cosmos, the force, universal energy, or New Age will never satisfy the quest for answers. Only the living God can do that. How do I know this? Because He has made it very clear to me in the person of Jesus, showing me in ways far beyond any earthly or religious realm of thinking. It is through that relationship with Him. He gives us a guide for living in one statement: Love God with all your heart; and love one another.

He is the only one who can be all things to all people. Each of us individually must seek the word of God—let it speak to our hearts—then walk the walk. Jesus tells us in John 8:12, "I am the light of the world. Whoever follows me will never walk in darkness, but will have the light of life."

Our lives were blessed even when we were going through hardships and stress. And who doesn't go through stress, especially with kids? We just had a different kid. But it wasn't until Jesus was part of my life that I really began to see how God was using Tim in the lives of those around him. Our memories of Tim are priceless, and without them we would have missed a tangible element of living proof that there is indeed a God.

> KELLY: Tim reminded me of the simple pleasures of life and of the truth that Jesus is real Love—real Joy—real Peace. I learned not just patience and kindness from a man whose legs carried him unsteadily through life, but of a determination and true devotion to God that helped steadily carry our spirits.

A Family Blessed

One morning as I was shaving Tim, I noticed his terribly bent spine and the long scar left from surgery when he was fourteen. There was a second scar where a large mole had been removed because it looked suspiciously like cancer. My heart was so filled with love for him. With tears streaming down my cheeks, I placed my hand upon his curved back and thanked God for my precious son just the way he was. No more looking for miracles, no more unrealistic prayers for healing. Simply, "Thank you for Tim, just the way he is."

That prayer was a release for me. I remember knowing at that moment Tim was already healed. This was the way God wanted Tim to be. I accepted that and was given an even greater peace.

In the Old Testament Abraham was tested by God. Abraham was told, "Take your only son, Isaac, whom you love, and offer him as a burnt offering." Abraham took Isaac to the place God had commanded. As Abraham was about to sacrifice his son, the angel of the Lord called to him from heaven and told him to stop. Abraham feared God and proved that he loved Him above all things, even above his only son.

Abraham was already close to God. He could hear God talking to him. But I believe that his spirit was never as close as the very moment he was about to offer up his son Isaac. Abraham's faith proved how much he loved God, and for that, the Bible tells us, his life was greatly blessed because of his obedience.

The word "sacrifice" means to offer up something precious. As a young mother, I wonder how I would have reacted if God had said to me, "I am going to use your son, whom I have created for a specific purpose, and it will be for My glory." In fact, that is exactly what God did when he sent us Tim.

Certain things came naturally to him, and his spiritual life headed the list. In the 1960s, Pat and I were involved in a religion class designed for the handicapped. It was the morning of Tim's first communion. Kneeling, head bowed, he looked up and told me he'd just asked God to forgive his sins. I can't remember discussing this with him. Maybe because he was retarded I didn't think it was necessary. The message of forgiveness and repentance certainly came through in a way that I missed. But then Tim didn't miss much, for God's Spirit was already working in his life.

Earlier I wrote about discipline and how important it is. We see results of kids today who do not have parents around and are not used to discipline in their lives. Society has bred generations of people who no longer take responsibility for their actions. Instead they blame everyone and everything else for their woes. The description of the word "woe" in the dictionary: overwhelming sorrow; grief, heavy affliction or calamity; disaster; to express sorrow; to denounce; or invoke censure; and misery.

Yes, we have become a woebegone world. Our young people and their parents experience all of the above. Because of Tim and the lessons he brought to our lives, Kathleen and Quinn received a broad education in life issues. Pat and I are grateful they and their families recognize and reach out to those who hurt physically and spiritually.

Both have a variety of memories growing up with Tim. One day when they were fooling around, Kathleen threw something and it hit Quinn between the legs. Tim told us Quinn got hit in the gallstones. And Pat's favorite is the morning when Kathleen came downstairs not feeling well and he asked what was wrong, why was she so crabby? She said she was sorry, it was only due to her period. Tim, standing close to her, gave her a shove and said, "Stay away from me—I don't want to catch it."

Written in my journal for May 13, 1978, eighteen-year-old Tim remarked, "Boy, what a cloudy day, but there's a lot of sunshine around here, Mom, because it's Mother's Day."

CHAPTER 8

A Real Survivor

August 24, 1983, age twenty-three: After Pat had a bad day Tim commented: "Look at the bright things, Dad, there's always a cloud before the sun rises."

Camp week arrived once again, and at age twenty-one, Tim was off to another great experience. Mark, a young man of 18, would be his attendant. Those seven days came and went much too quickly, and this week was no exception. In a blink of an eye it was time to pick up Tim. By now he would be exhausted from all the activities and late-night fun. Tim, Mark, and I walked to the car with a week's worth of dirty clothes and an assortment of goodies Tim won, made, or was given, and in his pack was another newly constructed stick house for Dad.

We were almost to the car when Mark asked me how old Tim was. "He's 21, why do you ask?" Somewhat embarrassed Mark's eyes looked to the ground, "I thought Tim wasn't telling me the truth." Now I was curious, "How old did you think he was?" His answer didn't shock me. He thought Tim was thirty years old. And we all know when we were 18 how we too thought being 30 was old.

Actually, Tim looked much older than 30. His face had developed deep crevices that come with aging and he was having more pain in his back and legs. I felt desperate to find a solution for this downward turn but concluded there wasn't anything we could do.

Pat and I could see him growing old in front of our eyes, and we couldn't stop it. He wouldn't be around too much longer if he kept going on this way. I prayed a very deliberate prayer asking for something to be revealed that would help Tim in all areas of his life. As I prayed, a thought came to me and I went directly to the phone.

My sister, Kathleen Piasecki, and her husband, Ray, lived close by in Antioch. Kathleen was a distributor for an enzyme product, and I remembered her telling us of its outstanding ability to help digest food. As we age, enzymes in our digestive tract become depleted, and food is not utilized or absorbed properly, leading to many physical problems.

This particular enzyme was first used on animals with amazing results. It was developed to help horses with colic, but also formulated for human consumption. Even though Kathleen, who was involved with the Humane Society, talked about them, I didn't give it a thought until now. I called and asked her to order us the Tyme Zyme Enzymes manufactured and distributed by Prozyme Products, Ltd.

Information on scientific research explained how these enzymes were proven to be stomach-acid stable. They digest food and aid in tissue repair, working like construction workers of the body. Without enzymes the biological process stops and the immune system and all other bodily functions are weakened. Tyme Zymes were to be taken with each meal, allowing vital nutrients to be absorbed by the body. They help replace naturally occurring enzymes lost during the cooking and processing of food.

Our package arrived and Tim began taking them. I didn't expect much; we were just trying something new. And besides, they wouldn't hurt. At the same time we couldn't imagine how anything might help reverse the aging that we saw. Could it help pain? Well, we'd see.

The curvature of Tim's spine was getting worse, increasing the need for medications, and sitting was becoming more uncomfortable. He took the enzymes for three days, and the terrible pain in his hips disappeared. He stopped complaining about his hips, back, and legs. With being on enzymes just one week, Tim was already referring to them as his "hip medicine." And this hip medicine was our answer to prayer. The enzymes were working!

Amazing Transformation

Changes in Tim became more and more evident. Every week we were seeing something new. He was standing straighter and energy levels increased. Normally he fell asleep in his chair around 8:00 in the evening, now he was able to stay awake until 10:00. With increased energy he was walking around, singing, doing things. He'd come into the family room to talk or watch TV with us. Naps in the afternoon were not a must anymore.

For the first time ever he was able to dial a phone, keeping all the numbers in proper order in his head. He repeated it to himself and completed the call. He was more alert in everything and greatly improved in taking phone messages.

To our surprise, in a very short time, the aged look of Tim's face reversed. His facial features looked young again. He didn't have to urinate as often and had less earwax, so his overall body was being affected in a very positive way.

Tim started on enzymes in July 1982. In October, Kathleen and Mark had a Halloween party and Tim was invited. He went dressed as Groucho Marx with heavy mustache and sideburns created with burnt cork. After the party, as I was washing off the blackened areas, I ran the cloth up into Tim's hair. "How on earth did you get this stuff in your hair?" I stepped back to look at him, and saw that his blond, graying hair had turned dark brown.

It happened overnight, and friends and relatives noticed the color change too. They were bringing it to our attention and kidded me about putting dye in his hair. At the same time, Tim was moving quicker, both in walking and getting up and down from a chair. He definitely felt better and had more patience, now noticeable to everyone.

In September of '82, I wrote to Prozyme Products to document the changes in Tim. A year later I sent a follow-up letter to inform them of ongoing changes during that second year.

Along with Tim walking faster, he was lifting gallon bottles of milk and apple juice and pouring his own drinks. He opened the car door easier. When Dr. Walter Sulkowski gave him his camp checkup, he looked at the palm of Tim's hand, then he looked at his own palm. He did this a couple of times. There was a puzzled look on his face, and I could see he was perplexed as he told me it was the first time he'd seen an improvement in the muscle tone of Tim's hand.

Dr. Sulkowski was a dear, kind man. He was loving and considerate toward Tim and always gave commonsense advice with lots of encouragement. Our trips to his office were pleasant events because I knew Dr. Sulkowski enjoyed seeing Tim. His office was small, quiet, and comfortable, and we felt as welcome as one could with a good friend. Mrs. Sulkowski was the receptionist, and because her husband donated a great deal of his time to children's programs, I know they did not send in the forms to get paid for Tim's visit.

Interesting Observation

Dr. John McMahon, a neurologist and volunteer for patients with muscular dystrophy, was the doctor provided for Tim at the MD clinic held at Evanston Hospital in Evanston, Illinois. He was Tim's doctor for twenty-one years. To sum it all up, after we related the many changes in Tim,

Doc McMahon, as Tim called him, gave an encouraging response. He told me he believed Tim had never absorbed nutrients through his food since birth. He felt we were able to see such changes because his body was now able to get nutrients through food and vitamin supplements. He told us to have Tim take all his vitamins with the enzymes to allow optimum absorption.

I could have hugged this man, but I was talking to him over the phone. But he confirmed what I felt for a very long time. Tim was born deficient of nutrients—the enzymes proved it. The absence of them prevented him from absorbing valuable vitamins and minerals. Vitamins were never prescribed for me during my pregnancies with both Kathleen and Tim.

Tim's body stabilized for a good many years. Doc McMahon was able to get a slight reflex in one of Tim's elbows for the first time. Improvements, no matter how small, were blessings.

This book would not be complete without a tribute to Doctor John McMahon—a man with a sweet, gentle spirit and genuine concern for his patients. His years of volunteer time devoted to muscular dystrophy patients cannot be measured. It was always a pleasure to see him when we'd bring Tim in for his yearly checkups.

He, too, would give advice with the combination of expertise and common sense. We appreciated his uplifting attitude and encouraging remarks when addressing Tim's condition and in handling his medication. Doc McMahon is well known beyond the walls of Evanston Hospital, and those who work with him dearly love him as we do.

Symbolizing the nature of his lifetime dedication to helping others is the little black bag he carries everywhere he goes. Now weathered from years of active duty, it still serves him well for the small instruments used to measure an important part of good health—muscle tone and reflexes. I think everyone, and especially Tim, loved to see that little bag. We will always hold a special place in our hearts for this kindly doctor and "friend."

A Thirty-Six-Year-Old Angel

"Your eye looks even worse today. Does it bother you?" Every morning I could see the fleshy area around Tim's left eye looking more irritated. It was November 1996, and after a routine eye check, our concern was nothing more than the effects of pressure from sleeping on that side of his face. (Later we realized he was having seizures during the night.)

However, the doctor discovered a much more serious problem. An excess of spinal fluid had built up behind the optic nerve. It caused swelling to the degree where most people would have already gone blind or had a stroke. An MRI the following day detected a condition called hydrocephalus, an accumulation of watery fluid within the ventricles of the brain. The only correction for this condition is for a shunt to be placed in the brain to regulate and direct fluid away from the brain to be absorbed into the body.

The pressure from this condition affected Tim's face, which had begun to look puffy, making him appear much older than his 36 years. It was probably one of the reasons for the recent bout of seizures he was having, even while taking medicine that worked for twenty years.

Within two days surgery for a shunt was performed and everything went well. Tim, in the recovery room, was fully awake, talking and feeling amazingly chipper. What a relief to hear him ask the nurse if she had a dog, and how he would send her a card for Valentine's Day. Once he left recovery, we weren't prepared for what lay ahead.

It was already 7:00 P.M. when he was moved to a room. Tim had walked the floor all day in anticipation of having to have another operation. Pastor Paul McMinimy, who is also a good friend, came to pray with us, and this helped ease some of the tension as we waited for an operating room to become available.

We weren't advised what to expect and didn't know he was supposed to be awake after this kind of surgery. He might say a few words if we insisted he speak to us. But this was nighttime and he had an exhausting day. What does happen when one has brain surgery? The nurse didn't feel there was an urgent need, nor did the doctor on duty who we called in at 10:00 P.M. During the night we forced Tim to say a word or two—but something wasn't right.

By seven the next morning we knew something was terribly wrong. Doctors were making their rounds and our fears were mounting when they came into the room. They discovered Tim was paralyzed on one side. Even though his eyes were closed he could hear and react to their questions by moving his other hand. With panic force the team rushed him for a CAT scan that showed an enormous hemorrhage filled the entire side and top of Tim's head.

He was never a bleeder, so this was a surprise to everyone. For all the twenty-plus operations throughout his life, he never had a problem. Emergency surgery was done and the whole side of Tim's skull had to be opened to rid it of the blood. (We now know that vitamin E, which thins the blood, can cause abnormal bleeding during surgery and Tim had taken E that week.)

While Pat waited on the surgery floor, I stayed in the room and prayed Psalm 61 as if Tim were praying it for himself. "Hear my cry, O God; listen to my prayer. From the ends of the earth I call to You, I call as my heart grows faint; lead me to the rock that is higher than I. For You have been my refuge, a strong tower against the foe. I long to dwell in Your tent forever and take refuge in the shelter of Your wings. For You have heard my vows, O God; You have given me the heritage of those who fear Your name."

Our family friend and pastor, Don Sweeting, along with our children, were with us as the neurosurgeon explained how serious the situation was and the procedure for reattaching Tim's skull. He could not tell us if there would be brain damage, but felt Tim could recover perhaps 80 to 90 percent. During his sickest moments when he awoke from one of the necessary additional surgeries, all he said was, "I love God."

After seventeen days in intensive care and a total of four operations, complications with meningitis (an inflammation of the brain lining due to infection) and pneumonia, Tim returned home December 5. By December 18, he felt good enough to go to Grandma Minahan's yearly birthday bash.

Thanks to Tim's determination, he recovered with only a slight weakness in balance and walking. During those uncertain days of recuperation, one young doctor described Tim as a "36-year-old angel." Tim made caring for him easy as he thanked doctors, nurses, aides, and technicians for each procedure done on him and for him.

We read him verses from the Bible about God's love for us. It was comforting and a time of spiritual peace. We gave God the glory for Tim's recovery, and we were grateful for prayers from so many people from many parts of the country. We personally attest to the fact that God's grace is sufficient for all our needs, and that in our lives everything comes together through Him. Psalm 55:22, "Cast your cares on the Lord and He will sustain you."

During this recovery period, Tim needed more shunt adjustments. The morning after one of these procedures, we returned to the hospital to find him doing much better. Cathy, the nurse assisting him, was on the opposite side of Tim's bed, and as I looked at her I asked if he had been asking for us, a natural thing for him to do. She answered with a testy remark to the positive while she rolled her eyes as though he was a real mental case.

I looked at this display of insolence and said to myself, "This young woman needs to be enlightened. She needs to be introduced to the world of love and kindness." Her attitude with everyone around her spoke a thousand ugly words.

We talked to Tim like we always did. We loved him and we expressed it with kisses, hugs, and loving words. Our other normal response—we joked, laughed, and prayed with him. Very quickly I saw a contrite Cathy as she realized her error in judgment toward him.

As days passed, Cathy continued to be the one assigned to Tim's ICU care. My visits found her and Tim joking, laughing, and kidding around. Cathy, like so many others, had been sprinkled with Tim's magical "sunshine." Her irritating facial expression was gone. She'd been drawn into Tim's world and was now smiling and joyful.

One morning I arrived to find her extremely excited and bubbly. Tim had zapped her with one of his surprise questions, and she was almost doing flips. He asked her if she was pregnant. And she was! She hadn't told anyone, but was making plans to leave very soon to get married in another state. How could Tim possibly know? He knew she wasn't married.

Cathy could not get over this, and she loved every minute of it. She was able to share a secret with Tim and then me, and it changed her world even more. All three of us prayed together and talked about the Lord and His plans for her. We gave her a small wedding gift and a baby gift and then she was gone. We never saw her again, but God's timing is perfect, and He used sunshine on her shoulder to touch her hurting heart.

Caregivers Worth Their Weight in Gold

Tim made a remarkable recovery. His mind was just as sharp and quick as before. I asked Pat to do something for me and his comeback was, "In my home I'm king of the castle." I answered, "Then that means I'm the queen." Without a moment's hesitation Tim chimed in with, "No, Mom, you're just the pheasant! (meaning peasant)."

> AMANDA STEWART (granddaughter): There are so many things that remind me of Uncle Tim, but some of my favorite memories are when I would go with my Grandma to take him to the doctor. While we were in the waiting room everyone would think Grandma was my mom. Then we'd go for lunch down at the little gift shop/cafe.
>
> It was always an adventure, but on one particular afternoon we had a very interesting time getting Uncle Tim into the car. Grandma would usually put him in from the passenger side, and I would pull him over and in from the driver's side. That day he wasn't being so cooperative. As we attempted to get him into the car, he started yelling, "Help!" At first it wasn't very loud, but then he got louder and louder and as people walked by, they were staring at us.
>
> At this point Grandma and I were bent over laughing so hard, tears streamed from our faces. She was saying, "Timmy! Timmy, stop that, you're fine." But he just kept on yelling. We kept laughing. And people kept looking at us. When we finally got him into the car, he was fine, but it definitely added an interesting twist to that visit to the hospital!

I was back working two days a week at the Chain of Lakes Community Bible Church, and Pat was busy with his home design business. "Mr. Fix-it," Tim's name for Pat, had put his carpenter tools away after 20 years of "saw dusting" (anyone pounding a hammer and sawing wood). Because Pat's office is at home I was able to work part-time. Now he and I needed more peace of mind and felt it would be good to have a caregiver for Tim on the days I worked.

Kay Widrick, our Kelly's aunt, had a career taking care of the sick and elderly in their homes. When I called her about staying with Tim, she surprised me by being available the days we needed her. She filled Tim's days with playing the guitar and singing, reading the Bible, praying, watching the Cubs games, along with giving much-needed physical therapy.

Reliable caregivers are in demand. Whether the person needing care is an adult or a child, the need for a kind and understanding caregiver is essential. Some families never do find the right person, or any person at all.

Roger, one of Tim's buddies from camp, had amyotrophic lateral sclerosis or ALS (Lou Gerhig's disease). There was a time Roger did not have this disease, but years dealing with it had taken its toll and he had to rely entirely on care from others. He wasn't able to do anything for himself, but computer technology gave him the ability to write beautiful, informative, humorous letters. The stories he'd tell about camp experiences were priceless.

Roger was able to talk through his computer. He used his mouth and referred to it as a sip-and-puff switch (special software for the handicapped). He went on to explain, "Luckily I was able to have it fixed without too many hassles. I bought a different switch which is a sensor switch that can be used anywhere you have muscle movement. A finger, foot, forehead, and so on can be used. This should take care of the dry mouth and scratchy throat when using the computer for awhile."

Freedom Taken for Granted

Roger had a flare for writing and used sharp, descriptive language. Continuing from the letter above, he wrote:

> The bird has his freedom to fly throughout the house but he doesn't come in my room as often as before. It's because he enjoys going to the back porch and looking outside through the picture window at the multitude of wildlife in the yard.
>
> He is starting to peck at the plants and digs in the soil. Sometimes he would be covered in dirt with dead grasses hanging on him. He would then groom himself by flying from room to room and taking a bath in his water. Now that it is getting colder, we don't have the back porch door open as often and he'll have to find another place of pleasure to cure his curiosity. When he does visit my bedroom, he would fly in and out and would land on the speaker where he can view everything and sing a bit. I believe he wants to join the characters outside!

Maybe Roger, who was so imprisoned by his own body, enjoyed the bird for the freedom it had to fly wherever it wanted. What he wouldn't do to have the freedom of a bird!

Roger was confined in a way that we could never imagine. His mother had died and Roger needed caregivers for him while his dad went to work. Roger wrote how one young woman wasn't very sensitive to his condition and needs. She'd bathe him and leave the window open with cold air blowing on him. He would end up with a terrible cold and have a difficult struggle to get well.

In the book *Weavings*, Henri Nouwen wrote about a community of mentally retarded adults he had the pleasure of working with and befriending. Adam was a twenty-five-year-old man who could not speak, dress himself, walk, or eat without help, and Henri became his caregiver—friend—brother. Because of grand mal seizures and heavy medications, it would take hours each day for bathing, dressing, and feeding Adam—routine things we do in an hour's time.

It was through his association with Adam that Nouwen discovered what the love and inner peace of God was really all about. He received a peace that the world cannot give and gained a spiritual awareness that it is our heart that is made in the image of God.

Society looks upon an Adam, or Roger, or Tim as burdens. How much one can contribute is the measure in which the world judges worth. When understanding and kindness are shown to one who has nothing to give back, we can become the recipients of multiple blessings that can only be explained as a holy experience. Oh, but it doesn't stop there.

Nothing at all to give back? How narrow a thought! Surely this handicapped person is made of flesh and blood, has a mind with feelings, experiences pain and hunger and love—especially love. Doesn't everyone have the capacity to love back? Is God speaking to us through that handicapped person? Could it be Jesus Himself?

We should not be surprised to find that the world cannot comprehend how, in actuality, it's the caregiver who is on the receiving end. When love and patience are shown to one who seems to have nothing at all, we become the recipients of a sacred connection to God. Henri Nouwen found a quiet, inner peace that he did not know before. If we are so fortunate to have been given a glimpse into the world of the profoundly handicapped like Adam and Roger, our hearts are opened and we have the ability to hear God speaking. And not only do we hear the whispers of the Lord, but we can experience His holy presence.

Precious Privileges

In October of '87, we took Tim to Disney World in Florida. It was a special trip because he was with us, and as usual God allowed everything to work out perfectly. The travel, weather, and lodging were great. Normally this time of year was the rainy season, but it was beautiful and sunny every day. We had ordered a mid-size car, and when we arrived at the airport they didn't have any left. We needed a car large enough for Tim's wheelchair, and they gave us a Lincoln Town Car for the same price.

When we experience God working I can't help but remark, "Never surprised—always amazed!" That comfortable, roomy backseat was wonderful. The four-hour round trip to Miami Beach to see my brother Ken would have been a strain; the larger car made a difference.

Tim had a ball seeing the sights and seeing the shows; he enjoyed handshakes with Disney characters and loved getting a big hug from Snow White. As we discovered long ago, people in wheelchairs do have some advantages. They're usually given good spots to sit and often are the first to be ushered into a building or an event.

Performers and athletes are known to seek out the disabled, and Tim had the privilege of meeting numerous sports figures throughout his lifetime. Many times it was that wheelchair that opened doors. The Chicago Bears came to Antioch High School to play the faculty, and afterwards they invited him into the locker room and gave him a signed football.

An acquaintance, Jim Swiatek, gave Pat tickets to a Chicago Bears preseason football game with the St. Louis Cardinals to be held at Soldier Field in Chicago. His father worked for the Bears in their front office. Pat and Tim had seats on the field next to the Bears bench—and directly behind (of all things) the cheerleaders.

A trip to the restroom was timed just right. The game was in progress, so the halls were empty as they made their way. No one was around . . . except Walter Payton, who was sidelined because of an injury. Pat and Tim saw someone motioning to them; a closer look revealed it was Walter. He introduced himself and 20 minutes were spent talking to him. Another time at Cubs Park in Chicago, Ernie Banks came up to the bus we were on to say hello to everyone.

I couldn't write about Tim without mentioning his love for the Bozo Show. Like all kids from that generation, he grew up with this famous clown. Everyday without fail, musical fun and laughter came from Tim's room with the antics of Bozo, Cookie the Cook, Oliver, Mr. Ned, Frazier Thomas, Cudley Dudley the long-eared dog, and so many others. Ray Rainer, who was Oliver O Oliver, came to Shriners Hospital when Tim was there recovering from surgery.

The original Bozo Show aired weekdays 7–8:30 A.M. on WGN in Chicago. On September 11, 1961, a new hour-long "Bozo's Circus" aired at 12:00 noon. It became an instant midday tradition and succeeded in reaching several million ardent fans from all over the world.

Bozo tickets at that time were like gold, with a three—to four-year wait that moved up to eight years and more. John and Jan Steitz had extra Bozo tickets and asked if we'd like to join them and their sons John and Jeff. As we went into the studio, we became part of the lively circus along with its TV viewers, being billed as "the cast of thousands."

Ray Rainer saw us, and he remembered Tim from the hospital and called to him by name. John and Jan were moved by this unusual recognition from such a busy personality as Ray. We had great respect for Ray Rainer and the job he did, for it was obvious he loved every minute of it. Our treasured photos of Kathleen, Tim, and Quinn along with John and Jeff standing with several of those lovable characters are priceless.

Kent Graham and his father, Vic, are longtime friends of Deke Kiemle, a friend of ours from church. In 1992, Kent was drafted as quarterback for the New York Giants. After three years he spent a year with the Detroit Lions and two years with the Arizona Cardinals, and then went on to play for the Pittsburgh Steelers and Washington Redskins. Deke brought his friends to visit Tim while he was recovering from the brain surgeries in '97.

Kent is very tall and Tim was very impressed. Looking up to Kent he commented, "Boy, you're really big." Tim was remembered with mementos and notes from Kent, and a special commemorative-signed football rests atop a shadow box filled with precious Tim-things. We can't know or recall all those in the sports realm and beyond who crossed Tim's path through situations he found himself in with hospitals, school and camp, but for sure there were many.

Bozo's Circus with Oliver & Mr. Ned, 1967

Bozo & Cookie the Cook acting up for Jeff & John Steitz, & Tim, Quinn & Pat, 1972

The Weak Made Strong

Tim's outstanding personality only blossomed in a greater way after graduation. He was with family and other adults daily, and the mannerisms he picked up from kids at school slowly diminished. With this also came improved behavior and speech. I still marvel at what a surprise this was.

When in school, Tim needed everything that school could provide, including his association with friends. Now going on twenty-two, he just stepped into another phase of his life, and it was filled with adults and not classmates. Even us old folk pick up subtle mannerisms from others. I guess that's human nature.

Once out of school, visits with good friends were few and far between. Tim would talk to Mike Malloy on the phone and occasionally see Tim Mahoney, Rick Lange, and Len Peters. Len was the only one from school who was able to drive and have his own car. When he'd come for lunch he always brought a heavenly dessert loaded with whipped cream. Tim Mahoney and Mike Malloy were Down syndrome men, each with differing talents and loving personalities.

For many years I was involved with Stonecroft Ministries and traveled throughout Illinois, Wisconsin, Indiana, and Iowa speaking to Stonecroft's Christian Women's Clubs. Involvement in our local Christian Women's Club added the positive influence my life needed. In '87 I became a Bible Guide for Stonecroft Ministries and had a Bible study in our home. Tim was part of this as we met faithfully every

Wednesday night for six years. Everyone in my family by now had accepted Christ into his or her life through the Stonecroft Bible Studies. Kathleen and I were first when we studied the gospel of Mark together, and then Pat, Quinn, Kelly, my mother Gee Gee (Helen), my sister Kathleen, nephew Scott, his wife Shirley, and Tim. And Mark says he heard the "Sermon on the Mount" from his mother-in-law every time he and Pat came home for lunch. Mark, too, accepted Jesus as his Savior.

We Care was an organization that provided weekly activities for graduates from Laremont who enjoyed getting together for an evening of dancing and fun. But when their bowling night fell on the same night as Bible study, Tim said, "I'd rather be at your Bible study, Mom, to learn more about God."

We joined the Chain of Lakes Community Bible Church (nondenominational) where Kathleen, Mark, Quinn, and Kelly were already members. We went from being visitors to attenders to members. Pat, Tim, and I filled out separate applications for membership.

As Tim and I sat in his room, I read him the application questions and became excited in the way he was answering them. I asked, "Tim, how do you know so much about God?" He looked at me with that animated face and answered in a rather annoyed tone, "Well, Mom, did you forget, I've been at all your Bible studies?"

Even though Tim wasn't able to do lesson plans, he gained biblical knowledge by listening to Scripture being read and being part of lively discussions. He grasped what it was to know and love God, and to learn how much God loves us. He absorbed what he heard and was able to contribute with questions and answers. Romans 10:17: "Consequently, faith comes from hearing the message, and the message is heard through the word of Christ."

Tim especially learned how much God loved him. When the question on the application read, "Who is Jesus?" Tim's answer was simple and direct—"He is God." The elders read his answer and they, too, were impressed.

Among other application questions, two more of Tim's answers stood out. When asked, "What is the significance of Jesus' death?" He answered, "He got nailed on the cross and He died for our sins." And then, "Suppose you were to die tonight and stand before God and He were to say to you, 'Why should I let you into my heaven?'" Tim's answer was, "Jesus died for us, so our soul goes to heaven and we get a new body." I think these were amazing answers coming from an amazing young man. We became members on January 20, 1991.

Don Sweeting was our senior pastor, and whenever he saw Tim, he'd go out of his way to talk to him. Tim enjoyed being a member of this new church and was impacted as much as we were by a new, growing experience with the Lord.

Maybe it was because Tim lived with so much pain that he sincerely felt the pain of others and prayed for them. And praying was something he learned to do just like the rest of us. We learned by doing, and it was heartwarming when he and I became prayer partners together.

KELLY: Tim's questions and desires were never for obvious reasons. But with each was sincere, selfless love and consideration for others. The simple pleasures of love and joy in the gifts God gives us were enough for Tim. Although asking why at times, he still embraced life as a gift, living it to please his Jesus. When he prayed, I knew it was sincere and a glimpse of God in our presence.

One January day in 1989, Tim and I were discussing prayer and he told me, "Praying at night is like taking a sleeping pill." And you remember he prayed so long at bedtime that I had to say, "Stop!" So he was probably praying on his own and falling asleep doing it.

Sometime later he and I became prayer partners with Pastor Don along with a small group from church. We committed to pray daily for him, his wife Christina, and sons, James, Jonathon, and Joshua.

During this same period of time, a morning Stonecroft Bible Coffee also met in my home. Being that Tim took his lunchtime seriously, if the ladies lingered longer than he thought they should, he would stand at the door leading into the room and raise his arm to look at his watch. That not-so-subtle hint worked every time. I would see all the women get up to leave at the same time, not realizing they'd been given a signal. The only one who did not see him was his mother, as my back was to him.

Tim's last Christmas with Quinn & Pat

All us girls, Christmas 1998. Back: Kelly, Gee Gee, Kathleen, Patti. Front: Brittany, Natalie, Amanda, Bryana

Kelly & Quinn

Gee Gee's loving touch

Enjoying some time with Bob Conrad

Mark & Kathleen

Not a SOX helmet?

Kathleen gets a birthday kiss

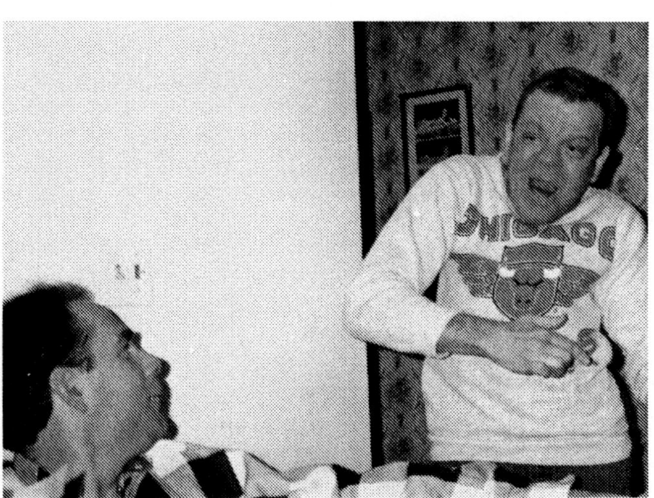

Typical of Mark and Tim

Tim with Kay at MD camp for the last time, June 1997.

With Mom . . . the way I will always remember him.

CHAPTER 9

So Many Prayers

One day Tim asked, "Dad, when you're dead, are you a spook?"

We looked upon Tim's recovery in '97 as truly a miracle, but weakness in his legs made it difficult for him to get into the car and cold weather was hard on his body. It was almost a year when we started leaving him home again by himself for short periods, knowing that a family contact was just a press of a button.

A regular greeting from Tim would be, "Happy first day of spring!" or "Happy Memorial Day!" or "Happy . . . anything!" He was always happy and he made us happy. It was January 25, 1998, "Happy Super Bowl Sunday!" Pat and I were getting ready for a trip the following week to renew old friendships at an army reunion.

After church we went shopping to get supplies for Kay and Tim. This was the first time we would be away and leave Tim with someone other than a family member, and I was happy how things were falling into place. After shopping we'd be home in time for the game. As we were about to head home I discovered I lost my new gloves and went back into the store to find them. Finally I gave up looking, I was becoming nervous and couldn't shake a feeling of urgency to get home—we were already gone too long.

With arms full of packages, we opened the door and as usual yelled out to Tim that we were back. When we didn't get an answer our hearts sank. We lived with the fear that we'd return home one day to find him unconscious or hurt. We rushed to his room and found him on the floor. He had fallen and hit his head on the wall. With eyes closed, the only thing he could tell us was that he fell asleep. I knelt and prayed, "Lord, please let him survive."

> NATALIE: When I think back to the many times I spent at my grandparents' house with my Uncle Tim, I remember a day I was doing my school work in the living room when a thought just popped in my head for no reason. My thought was, "What would I do if Grandma was upstairs and Uncle Tim fell right in front of me? Would I try to help him up myself or would I run to get Grandma?" I had decided I would run and get my grandma first.
>
> Right after I thought that, Uncle Tim fell in front of me, hitting his head on the wall and breaking his cane. My grandma was in the laundry room with the washer and dryer going so she didn't hear him fall. I ran to get

> her but she didn't hear me at first. When I told her again we both ran to help Tim. He had a cut on his nose and was so worried it would turn into a blister. Other than that, he seemed to be fine. I tried to be ready for just about anything that could happen to my Uncle Tim and it usually did.

He had fallen twice on Friday, once so hard that his cane broke. We wondered if that accident might have played a part in this fall. Pat knew immediately Tim was having another brain hemorrhage. It was on the other side of his head and massive by the time surgery was performed. As a result, we believe severe damage was done. The following week Tim was transferred to Evanston Hospital to be under the care of his regular neurosurgeon, Dr. Jeffery Cozzens.

Everyone was optimistic. We didn't give up, and certainly the doctors didn't give up. We were grateful for their positive attitude as they continued to work hard to stabilize Tim. But his brain reacted like a yo-yo, becoming dangerously swollen by overcompensating from one shunt adjustment, and then collapsing as a reaction to another.

Dr. Cozzens explained that Tim's brain did not adjust in the normal way. It went to extremes with each new shunt and reached the point where it simply could not take any more trauma. There wasn't any solution to be found, and he and his team were crushed. Tim's problems were unique, a real challenge for even an expert in his field.

As I look back, the progression of events are interesting. After Tim's remarkable recovery the year before, we made plans for him to attend camp with the Horizon group in

June. I took him to see Doc McMahon for his camp checkup. Not having heard from Roger in a long time, I asked the nurse how he was doing. She told me he had passed away a year ago, adding, "And he had a hard death."

I was deeply saddened to hear this news about poor Roger. I would have wanted to hear that he was spared any further hardship in his difficult life. But the curse of muscular dystrophy has not been lifted and it continues to invade the lives of many. With reflective thoughts about Roger, and in the quiet recesses of my mind, I remember saying to myself, "That will never happen to Tim." Well, here we were and it was happening to Tim. When he and I talked about death, he always told me he wanted to die in his sleep and I was confident the Lord would honor his request. But it was not to be.

Fear of the Unknown

It was February 24, 1998, and given that Tim was in the excellent care of ICU personnel, Pat and I went home to get a good night's sleep. But we were awakened by a call letting us know Tim was not responding after surgery done earlier that day. By the gravity of the message, we knew he was in very serious trouble and we could lose him. This meant another operation needed to be done immediately. The most horrible feeling came over me—I was not ready to let him go. With total anguish I prayed, "Lord, I am not ready, please don't take him from us."

Later the same day another quick surgery had to be performed, the third in a 24-hour period. This time his breathing was compromised and he had to be put on a ventilator. Three days later an attempt to take him off failed and he had to be put back on. Because of his weakened condition, and the fact that he had that severe scoliosis of the upper back, the process of having tubes put in again was probably detrimental to his overall recovery.

Two full weeks passed, and we were beside ourselves with worry and grief. For the three months Tim was in the hospital, Dr. McMahon made a point to come to Tim's room every day to see how he was doing. He too was having a hard time accepting Tim's downward turn.

We knew another attempt would be made to take Tim off the ventilator and were advised that if Tim couldn't breath on his own, they'd have to do an invasive tracheostomy. This is the placement of a mechanical ventilation tube into the throat. In most cases for people like Tim, it would be permanent. My dear friend, Jan Crane, who was a respiratory nurse, warned me not to get my hopes up, as the oxygen levels being monitored were not encouraging.

With this news, I began to pray differently. My focus was on God—on His sovereignty and on His victory over all things. I had reached the point where I could no longer bear Tim's suffering, nor could I bear his enduring a tracheostomy. Since Tim was retarded and had gone through so much already, deep within my soul, I knew he would not be able to withstand such a device.

The Bible tells us that God will not allow us to go beyond what we can bear. Many times He takes us down to the wire and then rescues us. From my experiences, that's exactly how He works in my life: taking me down to the wire to a place of brokenness and then releasing me with His peace. The verse from Proverbs 3:5 in the Old Testament says, "Trust in the Lord with all your heart and do not lean on your own understanding." I prayed with what I refer to as "full abandon," trusting Jesus in a way beyond anything I did before or since. It was prayer that I call abnormal, and the moving of the Spirit was almost tangible. And then it became tangible.

The respiratory team was ready. The doctor, attending physicians, and nurses entered Tim's room. They knew how upset we had been and could only remind me to "keep the faith." Little did they know what deep faith and trust my family and I have. I assured them I understood perfectly what the next step would be if taking him off the ventilator was not successful. And then I felt a blanket of comfort being wrapped around me as I walked away from Tim's room.

I purposely stayed in the hall sitting by myself, praying for what seemed like an eternity. My surrender was complete—full abandonment to God's will. After a very long half-hour the nurse came for me.

Walking back down the hall, I took a deep breath and asked, "How did it go?" "Oh just fine," she answered. Once again my favorite saying, when it comes to the faithfulness of God, immediately popped into my head. "Never surprised—but always amazed." God is so good. That precious time by myself, praying and trusting God—and the results were there for all to see.

Kathleen, Kay, and others began arriving. We were witnesses to a tremendous miracle. Tim's oxygen level was 100 percent. The special nurse assigned to watch Tim's progress for the first hour said it was very unusual to ever have such a high reading for anyone just off the ventilator. Tim was able to answer their questions with a strong voice, and his lungs were clear. Steroids were given three days prior to take the swelling down and the larynx was opened wide. Then the technician came in and read the levels on the monitor and muttered something about the numbers being "abnormally normal."

All of us stood around Tim's bed and gave God the glory through prayers of thanksgiving and songs of praise. Doctors and nurses were walking around with big smiles. How does one thank such a wonderful God! It was tangible!

A Broken Heart

My heart was broken—my soul was turbulent—my inner peace was gone.

The months passed: January 25 . . . February . . . March . . . April. Tim was still in ICU and his health was not improving. Even though he was off the ventilator, our hopes for Tim's recovery turned dim. Other complications set in, and except for the fact God honored our prayers regarding his not having to have a trach, Tim's condition deteriorated.

During these three and a half months, there were only three days when I was not at Tim's side. One day in April I came home to an empty house for a few hours of sleep. My heart was being tormented and there was an agitation of my soul. I realized, for the first time in twenty years, my spiritual peace was gone. From the moment I had accepted Christ into my life and had the burdens of a lifetime lifted from me, I was never without that peace—until now!

I sat in the corner of my dining room next to our glass door. Reaching for my Bible, I prayed and meditated on God's Word and asked Him to restore my spirit. I can't remember what I read but it isn't important. The Scriptures, bound in one book from Genesis to Revelation, are there for everyone. God's Word is alive and active and speaks to us today. I knew that was where I had to go.

Within minutes His loving peace flowed through me once again like a comforting drape covering me from head to toe. The facts hadn't changed. Tim wasn't any better and the future looked grim. Pat and I and the rest of our family were still in deep despair. Everything remained the same. But I was filled with the Lord's peace, centered in the heart, and it overflowed my whole being. Psalm 34:18, The Lord is close to the brokenhearted and saves those who are crushed in spirit, and 147:3, He heals the brokenhearted and binds up their wounds.

I never came closer to God than when we as a family needed Him the most—and He was silent! God was silent in Tim's time of need for health and recovery—so very, very silent. But through that silence the Creator of the universe expressed His love and allowed us to see His almighty power. We experienced and felt His presence in a way that I can't put into words.

After 10 operations and unforeseen complications, we brought Tim home on May 6. We worked with him in a positive way to help him recover whatever the Lord was going to allow. From beginning to end we had no one to compare his situation with. There were no other Tims out there for us to know what to expect. What should we do?

Relatives and neighbors brought food, and families from church provided meals for weeks while we cared for him around the clock. I don't know what we would have done without them. Nurses and a physical therapist came into our home for several weeks, but progress was at a standstill. Tim was absolutely void of any facial expression. That smiling, animated face we loved so much was now blank. We could see the situation had become hopeless. What a terrible place to be.

> NATALIE: My mom home-schooled me so I was able to go with her to help take care of Uncle Tim and help out my grandparents. The last five-and-a-half months of his life he couldn't talk or do anything for himself. I made up a bag of things that I thought might help him get better. I brought a flashlight that I had him turn on and off with his finger and used cards to see if he could match them up, but he couldn't. I brought coloring books and was able to prop a crayon in his fingers and we'd try to color together. I would read to him, but would get very little response. He always loved to mark each day off of his calendar so I'd try to help him put an X on each day. Everything was really hard for him.

Where are you, Lord? And what on earth are you doing? Tim was accustomed to pain and suffering all of his life. Now we were experiencing what I referred to as "the pit of hell," watching him in a life struggle I never thought he'd have. All normal reasoning had gone out the window.

Tim went from doing just about everything for himself to one day waking to find himself imprisoned in his own body. He wasn't speeding in a car or hurt riding a motorcycle. He didn't drink, smoke, or take drugs. He wasn't in a dangerous environment that would cause his not being able to speak, eat, walk, or use his arms or legs. Everything, limited as it had been, was taken away. He was at the mercy of others. Not only was it despairing for him but humiliating as well.

Pat and I could not have cared for Tim alone. The job was overwhelming. When we brought him home, Kathleen had just completed an obligation in helping another family in a situation that was also beyond their control. Julie, a young mother, died of cancer, leaving her six-month-old infant daughter, Sarah. Her father Dave needed someone to care for her while he worked, and Kathleen, Mark, Amanda, and Natalie became part of her family. Now at the age of two-and-a-half, Sarah and Dave moved back to his home state. This happened the day before Tim came home.

> KATHLEEN: One of the greatest privileges of my life was to help take care of my brother those last two months of his life. Because I was home-schooling my younger daughter Natalie, we were available to help with Tim.
>
> When Sarah first came into our lives I was overwhelmed with the thought of loving this precious little girl but

> knowing someday she would be gone. It might be when her dad remarried or if they were to move to her father's family in Pennsylvania. I cried and prayed, 'Lord, what am I going to do, and how am I going to handle it when you take Sarah away?' Instantly, I was filled with a sweet peace, and I heard an unmistakable inner voice assure me that He would take care of Sarah—He would take care of me—and He would have something else for me to do. From that time on, I fully allowed myself to love Sarah without worrying about the outcome. I did wonder, though, what it was that He had for me to do?
>
> My family and I returned from a short trip the same day Sarah and her dad returned from a trip to see his family. Dave told us they would be moving to Pennsylvania. It was heartbreaking to lose this little ray of sunshine that had become so much part of our lives, but I clung to the promise the Lord gave me two years before. The day after Dave and Sarah left, we brought Tim home from the hospital. He was critical and needed 24-hour-a-day care. I remember standing in my kitchen crying and realizing that this was the other thing the Lord had for me to do.

God's timing is perfect. Kathleen then put everything aside to be here for Tim and for us. She and Kay Widrick were faithful to the end. And Natalie, being home schooled, was part of this caring team, working with Tim in many different ways trying to get him to respond.

Jean Heggen, a friend from church and experienced in Hospice, volunteered to come the mornings that Kathleen and Kay weren't here. With her sweet, quiet spirit, she was yet another blessing the Lord allowed us when we needed it so badly.

> KATHLEEN: It was a joy and a privilege to love and care for Sarah. I asked God to fill me with the same joy for taking care of Tim, even with having to change his diapers and feed him with a stomach tube. I also realized that the Lord was teaching both Natalie and me far more than anything we could learn through books. The blessings were innumerable.

We accepted all assistance offered and would not have survived the daily strain if it weren't for family and friends, but we did it. The Lord provided, and with help we hung in there and completed the job God had given us to do. And yes, I believe with all my heart that God gave us this precious job and the responsibility to see it through to the end. This awesome experience awakened us to the fact that we can never forget how people all around us, for that matter all around the world, are enduring the same trials and heartaches.

This morning I received a message from a tearful young woman named Tammy. She called to let me know her twenty-one-year-old brother, Matt, had passed away in his sleep. The Lord stretched out his hand to him in the middle of the night—no more pain, no more tears. His family was preparing for that moment, lovingly guarding and watching.

Matt was one of those "special people" I talk about. He also knew Jesus as his Savior and his heavenly reward was being prepared, and when it was ready, God called him home. Just being with the Lord is our great reward. But for Matt, I know the blessings of heaven will be far greater because of who he was.

A year ago, Pat and I were introduced to his mother, Sandy, by my sister Kathleen and husband Ray. They felt because of Tim, we could be of some comfort to her. Matt lived with an inoperable brain tumor since he was eight years old, but mentally he was only the age of six. He was homebound and needed his spirits lifted as his overall health was beginning to deteriorate.

Pat suggested we print his name and address in our church bulletin so notes and cards could be sent to him. People responded and Matt was flooded with mail. As time went on, the mail slowed down, but I continued to send letters along with printed information about airplanes. I wish I had thought of this for Tim, who would have loved to get encouraging mail.

It was two weeks ago that I finally met Matt, and I regret not meeting him sooner. Just being with him filled me with the same spiritual connection—that same good feeling I had when I was with Tim. It's what I miss so much. It is their sweet dependence on others and the fact that you know you will never be able to do enough.

With all that is covered in this book, I need to add one more thought, and that is to encourage everyone to reach out to those who are disabled with visits, calls, cards, and notes. Most will have their time here on earth cut short. What they are able to do, they do with a lot of help from others as they look to them for their survival.

MARK: I don't know if God gives special-needs children to special parents, but from what I've seen, Tim couldn't have had more loving parents. They didn't baby Tim as a young man, but let him grow to be himself—his own thinker and his own special person. All kids should be so lucky to have loving parents like Patti and Pat. It was really a privilege to get to be a friend of Tim.

Our Plans Are Not God's Plans

Before I began to write this story, I decided to focus on what is encouraging and elevating. My purpose is to amplify and share the many blessings we derived from having a special child. Tim taught us what life is all about and how to be tough and strong during times when we could neither influence nor hold sway over a particular situation.

To communicate details of all that Tim went through and experienced would defeat the purpose for this book. My intentions are to reveal how God blessed us with the positive and the good; the loving and the spiritually uplifting. And I know Tim wouldn't want it any other way.

I also want to remind you that the vast majority of people suffering hardships and disabilities began their lives robust and healthy. And in my mind, the argument about those mentally and physically disabled not contributing to our elite society does not hold water. They do indeed have a special place here, and God uses them to touch the hearts and lives of the people around them. As I look back and see what has transpired down through the years, my question is, *what would we do without them?*

For the length of time Tim needed us during his last days, Pat and I were given abnormal amounts of energy, strength, and stamina that could only have come from the Lord. I never had to take as much as an aspirin during Tim's extended hospital stay. I never had a headache or the bodily aches and pains that accompany my fibromyalgia.

Everything we needed was given to us. Balanced meals, safe travel, my sister Sharon's home to stay at night close to the hospital, and the love and encouragement from family and friends both near and far. Pastors Don and Paul were spiritual lights during our dark voyage.

We experienced what it means to be part of a loving church family. Chain of Lakes Community Bible Church was there for us from start to finish, filling areas of need and holding us up in prayer. We are indebted to so many for all their help in a time when each morning we'd wake up with the same sick jolt of disbelief.

Our friend Dr. George (Doc) Sweeting came to visit Tim on one of those warm summer days. It was the latter part of June and Tim was sitting on our screened porch with Kay. Pat and I were home, and we welcomed Doc and the heartfelt warmth only he can bring. His contagious smile, with soothing words and prayers, was good medicine for all of us.

We appreciated him being here as his busy schedule takes him all over the world. Doc Sweeting has been at Moody Bible Institute in Chicago for over twenty-five years, first as president and then as chancellor. Doc is Don Sweeting's father.

In the morning I began putting on the Moody Christian station, WMBI (90.1) out of Chicago, and there was a marked change in Tim's comfort level. The joyful voices and spiritual messages were soothing, and this amazed me because we tried musical stations and musical tapes. He'd also hear Doc giving his devotional on his regular daily broadcast, *Climbing Higher*.

Doc is familiar with those who hurt physically and spiritually and has ministered to thousands of people in his lifetime of service to the Lord. He himself overcame cancer years ago as a young man and knows personally what it's like to experience healing and answered prayer from a faithful God.

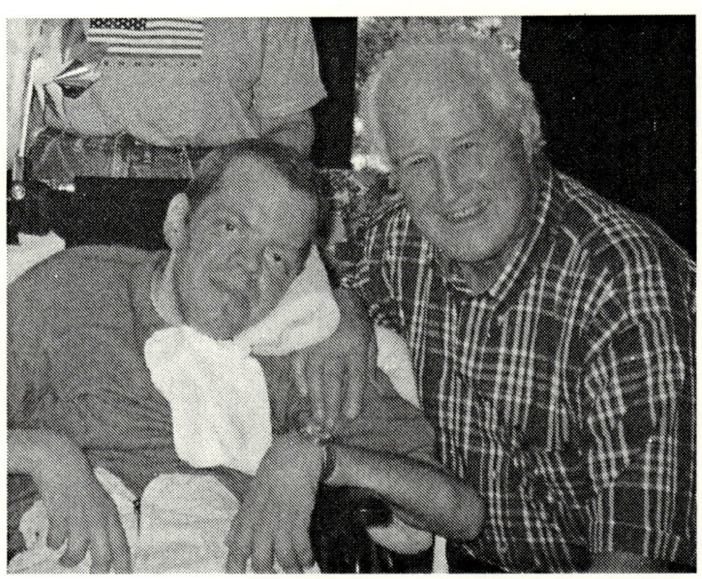

A blessed & timely visit from friend, Doc (George) Sweeting

A Special Birthday

Tim was thirty-eight on January 30, five days after that fateful Super Bowl Sunday. We celebrated somewhat while he was in the hospital, but as weeks passed we realized he was not remembering what had happened the day before. Because of this, he thought he was still thirty-seven.

A July 4 birthday celebration was planned to officially declare him thirty-eight, and it began with a parade in Antioch. Tim was alert and able to wave a little flag at the colorful floats. We went home to where family and friends gathered for a marvelous party. Red, white, and blue streamers decorated our screened porch, and matching balloons were everywhere.

Typical of Tim, he always rose to the occasion, and on this day he rallied from the depressive and tearful state he had been in. He was awake all day, opened presents (with help), looked at cards, interacted, and talked a bit. He even had a small taste of ice cream and cake.

The next day, Sunday, he continued to do better, and our spirits were uplifted. All of a sudden he put his hands on the arms of his wheelchair and lifted himself up to a better sitting position. I yelled to Pat who came running. Tim couldn't hold his head up anymore, so we put a pillow on his shoulder to support his head. To witness him moving and lifting his body like he did gave us another glimmer of hope. I took him outside to our deck where it was sunny and warm and helped him stand for a minute or two as he held onto the railing.

Then at 3:00 A.M. Monday I went to change him and he began gasping for breath. I hugged him and told him to relax, that everything would be okay, but it only got worse. The rescue team arrived minutes after our call—and I'm still wondering how they got here so fast. They were surprised Tim was still conscious because of the low registered oxygen level. They gave him oxygen, and once again we found ourselves in the emergency ward. Nothing more could be done, and Hospice prepared our home for Tim to return the next day, Tuesday. The Lord had guided us through the storm and directed our spirits to the place where we were ready to let him go.

The time had come. Lovingly, softly, we whispered: "Tim, it's time to go to be with Jesus." We reminded him that in heaven he'd have the new body he looked forward to, something that he and I had talked about for years. It was now going to be a reality for him. We played spiritual music, said prayers, and had friends and relatives in his room all day Tuesday until late Wednesday night.

> NATALIE: I remember the week my Uncle Tim died. It was like a big family reunion. It seemed like hundreds of people came over to see Tim for the last time. He was in a coma and very peaceful. My mom and sister and I, with my Aunt Kelly, Uncle Quinn, and my cousins all spent the night. The next morning at 7:00 A.M. my uncle died. The day before he died I had gone outside to cry, and sat in the yard. My mom came out to sit with me. Just then a brown rabbit came up very close to us and sat down and looked right at us for several minutes. It turned and peacefully hopped away. I love animals, and it seemed to be God's way of comforting me.

It wasn't a surprise that our family was with us to be close to Tim and close to one another. Everyone spent the night. Kathleen and Mark, with their daughters, Amanda (fifteen) and Natalie (eleven), and Quinn and Kelly, and their daughters, Brittany (eleven) and Bryana (eight). Quinn and his girls slept on the floor next to Tim's bed and watched over him during the night.

Thursday morning, July 9, followed a restless night. We were surprised to find Tim's heartbeat was strong and steady. I began my usual routine and told him I was going to shave him as I did every morning at 7:00. He knew I loved to shave him and how special it was for me. Pat would kid him and ask who gave him a better shave, and he would always say, "Mom, because you always leave particles."

Pat and Quinn stood alongside his bed, and as I shaved the last of the stubble, they both realized at the same time that Tim's heart had stopped. The beat of this strong, steady heart that Quinn examined just moments before simply stopped. After a heroic five-and-a-half-month struggle, Tim was called from this life and entered into the presence of the Lord.

Kathleen prayed for me to experience something special before Tim passed away. And when I heard that, I wasn't surprised that he waited for me to shave him. It was as though he felt, "I waited for Mom to shave me, now I'm ready to go." For Kathleen, her prayer was answered. . . . And for me? I was given a spiritual memory to be treasured always.

Death for Tim brought us to the ultimate awakening in what life is all about. This is the highest achievement in one's life. Tim was no longer of this world. He was now at the place where the welcoming arm of Jesus ushered him into a glorious, eternal life.

It's difficult for me to even think back on what a blessed experience this was for our family. Tim was with the Lord. The months of unanswered prayer came together, and now they were answered. I can't explain this either, but in my heart, they were answered.

The atmosphere in the room was filled with love and peace as we encircled Tim. He was probably looking down on us wishing he could tell us all how much he loved us. It was a time of thanksgiving as we praised God through prayers and hymns. We rejoiced for Tim; he was at peace—we were at peace. No more pain or tears for Tim, but our pain and tears would continue. Like Tim, that final day awaits us all. The finality of life as we know it will surely stare each one of us in the face. And with that I ask, are you ready?

Citizenship in Heaven

> NATALIE: I'm so happy I was able to go with my mom to help take care of Uncle Tim. I know someday I'll see him healthy and happy in heaven. I'm looking forward to that day.

God's heavenly hand touched us in very dramatic, down-to-earth ways—ways that could not be denied came directly from a holy presence that allowed Tim's love for us to be made known.

For Father's Day, Tim had given Pat an alarm clock for his office. Pat wound it, set the correct time, and placed it near his desk. Days, maybe weeks passed and it wasn't noticed. When Pat looked at the clock just a couple of hours after Tim died, the clock had stopped at 7:00. While at Tim's side the moment his heart stopped, Pat looked at his watch. It was 7:00 o'clock.

The day after the funeral, Pat and I were talking about Tim being in heaven—about the Lord's promise to those who know Him as their Lord and Savior. At the same moment, we received an amazing confirmation as I reached for the *One Year Bible* next to my bed. There it was as big as life. With utter amazement, I read out loud the Scripture reading for Thursday, July 9.

With the title, *Citizenship in Heaven,* I began reading Philippians 3:17–21 from the New Testament, verses 20 and 21: "And we eagerly await a Savior from there, the Lord Jesus Christ, who, by the power that enables Him to bring everything under His control, will transform our lowly bodies so that they will be like His glorious body." How faithful the Lord is in giving us a very clear message through His written word. Never surprised—always amazed!

Later that week I noticed someone had turned the daily Scripture on my bathroom shelf to July 9. It's from Job 22:21 (RSV) and reads, "Agree with God and be at peace; thereby good will come to you." I cannot express how much this verse means to me as I apply it to every situation we encounter.

When all is said and done, life becomes easier to bear when we make a conscious effort to "agree with God." His grace *is* sufficient for *all* situations.

Our precious son left this world but not without touching the lives of all who knew him. Our family was blessed to have Tim for thirty-eight years. And the world is a much better place because Tim was part of it.

> QUINN: I get a head cold and I'm dying. Tim gets a life-altering, crippling disease, and he lives more in his thirty-eight years then I have in my almost forty years. And he's more alive now then he's ever been.

CHAPTER 10

Apostle With a Cane— July 13, 1998 Philippians 1:6, 9–12, 20–26

"Hey, Dad, if I were okay, do you think I would be a good father?"

"Yes, Tim, you would be a wonderful father."

The energy level that was so high all day had begun to wane. It was 5:00 P.M., and Pat and I were weary and exhausted as we sat on our screened porch with Anna Mae and Bob. The mood was quiet and reflective. And it was as it should be. We had just returned from Tim's funeral service of Celebration and Thanksgiving. It was part of an ongoing sequence of events that began thirty-eight years ago, and now we were experiencing the closing chapter.

Don Sweeting had already accepted a new pastoral position in Colorado, and with some incredible last-minute arrangements, he was able to fly back for Tim's service.

Don and Paul McMinimy officiated at the service, with Don giving the eulogy entitled "The Apostle with a Cane." He used the writings of Saint Paul to illustrate the bondage of prison that Paul dealt with and the physical and mental prison Tim Stagg had to deal with. Tim had been a prisoner of muscular dystrophy and all of the other hardships he lived with. But none of these experiences was in vain when we trust God and His sovereignty in our lives.

> PASTOR SWEETING: Once in a while a book is published with a title so intriguing that you have to open it. That's how I felt when I saw a book written by D. James Kennedy entitled, *What If Jesus Had Never Been Born?*
>
> Think of Christ's impact on world history, on education, on the family, on economics, on health and medicine, on science, on the settling and founding of the United States, on morality. Think of the encouragements and restraints brought to our civilization through the influence of Christianity. And think of all the lives changed by Jesus Christ! Had Jesus never been born, our lives would be immeasurably poor.
>
> Let me pose another question. What if Timothy Patrick Stagg had never been born? Our lives would be much poorer. Tim was born into trouble like the rest of us, but he was born into more troubles than we would wish on anyone. And yet Tim's life had a huge impact on many.
>
> I have many memories of Tim: meals at his home, family gatherings I was invited to, his visits to our home! He was at church often. And I remember stories about

his wild times at camp. As a lover of baseball and a New York Yankee fan, I remember coveting his baseball signed by Babe Ruth!

More importantly, Tim was one of my prayer partners who prayed for me and my ministry. Surely you have your own stories of Tim. The long and short of it is Tim was a blessing to many!

Let me go further. Tim's life is a sustained argument that the abortionists and euthanasia proponents are wrong. Life's value and quality cannot be measured by physical handicaps alone. Often we discover that the value of those handicaps is much greater than we ever imagined! They become God's special means to do God's special work.

Unfortunately, many people only see a life like Tim's as an inconvenience to be avoided at the outset. Had Tim been born in the 1990s to another American family, he'd be lucky to get past birth! Things were different when Tim was born . . . as God put him in a family that viewed human life through God's eyes. Tim was welcomed and cared for with a deep compassion for all of his thirty-eight years.

I'd like you to think of Tim as the apostle with a cane. Can you picture him walking with his cane?

I noticed parallels in Philippians chapter one between the Apostle Paul's role with those at Philippi and Tim's role here in the Chain of Lakes. Paul of the New Testament is often referred to as "the apostle in chains" because he wrote the Philippians while in a Roman prison. Tim, I submit to you, was the apostle with a cane. Let me show you what I mean. Paul an apostle, meaning messenger, was sent by Christ on a mission as His spokesman.

Tim's mom reminds us that, "The Lord used Tim to bring us to a saving knowledge of eternal life in Christ." He was not the founder of a church, like a New Testament apostle, but he was still a messenger sent from God. He was, if you will, an apostle in disguise. God in His sovereignty used Tim and his troubles to bring the Stagg family to the feet of Christ. He used Tim to bring them to faith, to dependence, to their knees before the Lord. Tim was, in Patti's words, "an ambassador from heaven." In my words, "the apostle with a cane."

Paul's prison experience actually furthered his ministry. While in chains, he writes that there are even saints in Caesar's household. Certainly Paul had a captive audience day in and day out when he was either in a room with, or chained to, one of Caesar's elite guards.

Tim had his prison too. His body was a prison, and the cane is a reminder of this. He was born with a defect of the lower spine, underdeveloped legs, was mentally retarded and later developed muscular dystrophy.

God uses the hard things of life to bring blessings. In fact, I suspect that Tim gave more to us with his troubles than he would have had he been a hotshot athlete. There are many whys. Why does this one suffer and not that one? Why this family and not that one? Nevertheless, we do know that Tim's troubles worked for the blessing of many. That is the way it often is with our prisons, or chains—or canes!

By the middle of the first century, Paul's chains were gone forever! His work was over. God called him home. In his late thirties, Tim's prison is gone forever. His canes will be left behind. When his work was done, he departed to be with Christ, which is better by far!

The day before his death, Patti told Tim, "It's time to let go and be with Jesus." She summarized, "What peace we have in knowing where Tim is, no more pain and tears. We have God's assurance that we will see him again." That is exactly right, for the Christian.

In his final days, Patti asked Tim if he prayed to Jesus. He said, "Yes." She asked if he talked to Jesus. He said, "Yes." Then she asked him if he *saw* Jesus. And he said, "Yes."

Paul explains what happens to the Christian at death. In 2 Corinthians 5:6–8, he tells us that the situation of the Christian before his death is, "We are at home in the body but away from the Lord." While we can experience the nearness of God all through this life, this nearness is nothing like the nearness we shall experience when we see Him face to face.

Then Paul reminds us that, for the Christian, after death is "Away from the body and at home with the Lord." According to the Bible, in 1 Corinthians 15, the believer who dies immediately enters the presence of the Lord. He is glorified, that is, complete in Christ and fully united with Him. The heart is set free from all sin. The saints in heaven, in the presence of Christ, will receive glorified bodies on the day of resurrection.

Paul tells us to find our peace and provision in the Lord. In Philippians 4:6 we read "Do not be anxious about anything, but in everything, by prayer and petition, with thanksgiving, present your requests to God. And the peace of God, which transcends all understanding, will guard your hearts and your minds in Christ Jesus." He adds, "And my God will meet all your needs according to His glorious riches in Christ Jesus."

Thank God that Tim Stagg had been born. He was a beloved brother, a precious son, a dear grandson and easy friend, a faithful prayer partner, a wise and simple man, even a "dancin' machine." He was for some of us, the apostle with a cane. May God continue to use this ambassador of heaven to bring you to the feet of Christ.

A Blessing from Heaven

Our celebration of Tim's life was shared with a church full of people who blessed us with their presence and their love. Kelly, her Aunt Kay, Pat's brother, Gus (Glenn), and Christina Sweeting drew us into worship with music. Sweet heavenly sounds flowed from the piano and violins of Kristin and Tracy Figard. And with the sun shining brightly, we all felt the warm touch of sunshine on our shoulders.

Anna Mae, Bob, Pat, and I began to reflect on all that had happened. Pat talked about how guilty he was going to feel now that we would be able to do things we weren't able to before. I knew exactly how he was feeling, I, too, was wondering how much of an adjustment it would be for us. All of us agreed it would take time to get over not putting Tim first before everything else.

I don't know what prompted me to leave the three of them, but I found myself standing at the entrance to our family room. Thoughts of Tim . . . Then I noticed a large, heavy, wooden plaque that hung at the peak of a ten-foot wall for the past twenty-three years had fallen onto our couch. Pat and I were the only ones in the house before we left; it must have fallen during Tim's funeral. Placing the plaque on the table I rejoined them on the porch.

The plaque laid on the table for a couple of days when it came to me that there were words written on it. Even though they were in Scandinavian, one was plainly the word "God." So we took it to Scandia House, a restaurant we frequent often, and asked Jenete Martens to translate it. As she read—"Eat, drink, and be glad—thank your God for every day"—we knew it was a message for us to hear.

That plaque was used to bless us, as the message addressed our feelings. We no longer needed to worry about Tim; those times were now in the past. We could go on with our lives without feeling guilty. The same words are found in the Old Testament book of Ecclesiastes 9:7.

As I related this discovery to Kathleen, she told me that Ecclesiastes 9:7 was the verse she had read in her daily devotional for Thursday, July 13, the day of the funeral. Her version ends with, ". . . for God has already approved your works" (NASB). Another coincidence? Not a chance.

For twenty-three years the plaque hung directly over a narrow shelf. On the shelf immediately below the plaque were two items: an old-fashioned heavy black iron and a heavy primitive clay container. The more I studied the space the more I questioned how that plaque could have passed between them without touching or moving one or both. It would have had to fall directly onto the shelf first before landing down on the couch.

My curiosity would not be satisfied so I measured the space. I took the plaque up to the shelf to replay its path from wall to couch. Whether it rolled to the right or left of the shelf, or just fell forward, there is no way it could have dropped off without moving something or knocking a piece off. My granddaughter Amanda said it best, "An angel took it off the wall for us to have." What else can I say except, "Amen."

April Nelson and her two young daughters, Abigail and Annette, were at Tim's funeral. A week or so later, she and the girls joined her husband Bruce who was working in Morris, Illinois. Bruce and our son Quinn were friends from high school, and Bruce's brother Charles and Tim were very close buddies and classmates at Laremont School.

While in Morris, April took her girls to the hotel pool. She began talking to a man named Moose from Whiting, Indiana, who had his kids swimming there too. In their conversation, Moose told her he works with muscular dystrophy people at a summer camp. When April asked him where the camp was, he said Hastings in Lake Villa. Her next question, "Do you know Tim Stagg?" Moose said he certainly did know Tim and went on to tell her how they named a dance after him, and added, "But he wasn't at camp this year." Then April told him she had been to Tim's funeral and gave him her program of the "Celebration" service.

Pat and I remember meeting Moose many times, and also heard Tim talk about him and his other camp friends. Morris, Illinois, is over a hundred miles away from Lake Villa. And Whiting, Indiana . . . ? A coincidence?

> KATHLEEN: Three weeks before Tim died, the pressures of watching him struggle for life stretched our nerves thin. We were on edge without a release—each of us drowning in our own personal grief. Much of it was silent as each day was a disheartened repeat of the day before. My folks virtually went without sleep and were able to eat only because people were bringing meals for them.
>
> My dad and I, in a confused moment of misunderstanding, had the worst blow-up we have ever had and hurt feelings I thought were gone surfaced. The next day, as we both asked each other for forgiveness, the Lord did a wonderful healing of the hearts. When I shared what happened with my younger brother Quinn, there was even more healing, and expressions of love replaced our sibling resentments. I felt, Tim can go now. His purpose for hanging on has been fulfilled.
>
> I would never trade my family for anything. The incredible memories, both good and bad, have been life lessons. I realize, because of Tim, our family sees things differently than most people. Hopefully we are more sensitive to those around us. We do not see people so much as different or weird, but unique. God blessed our family so richly when He allowed us the awesome privilege of being Tim's family.

KELLY: As I remember the many ways Tim touched all of us, somehow I cherish his questions and walking lessons the most. They reveal what God might ask me, to ask myself, serving as a reminder how I might experience the Lord more in "my walk." If someone asked me today, was Tim a good example of a man who was truly made in the image of God? I would have to smile, and reply as I always did. . . . "The best, Tim was . . . still the best."

Fragrance of Fresh Flowers

Over and over again I would tell Tim how much I loved taking care of him. I made it clear it would be much better if he could take care of himself like he used to, but because he couldn't, I loved being there for him. One of my great personal sorrows is not being able to take care of him anymore. He was our life—a special companion to Pat and me.

I would look at Tim in his final days and wonder if God had not already taken him from this place. The few times we heard Tim talk is when the words just came out automatically. What he'd say would be quick and short, and if we asked him to repeat it he couldn't.

He told me and then Pat that he wanted to go home. We replied that he was home . . . but we now believe he wasn't talking about his earthly home. When I looked at Tim I imagined it could be Jesus, Himself, I was caring for. That thought caused me to reflect. . . . I might well be caring for the Lord here and now.

A year and a half passed when Pat and I were talking about flowers. I never shared with him that while Tim was still here, I'd go into his room and smell the most beautiful fragrance of fresh flowers. I remember looking around the room to find the source of that sweet bouquet but never found anything.

I was awestruck when Pat revealed he had the exact same experience. He would go into Tim's room and wonder where the beautiful scent of fresh flowers was coming from. For some reason we just never mentioned it.

In Song of Solomon 2:1, the verses "I am the Rose of Sharon. . . . I am the Lily of the Valley," illustrate the beauty and sweetness of Jesus. These beautiful, sweet-smelling flowers are representative of the Lord and His love for us. They reveal how the brightness of His beauty becomes a holy fragrance to those who know and love Him.

We in turn can become a holy fragrance to Him. Second Corinthians 2:14–15 tells us, "But thanks be to God, who always leads us in triumphal procession in Christ and through us spreads everywhere the fragrance of the knowledge of Him. For we are to God, the aroma of Christ. . . ."

God allowed Tim to be a sweet fragrance with which to influence the world around him. He completed his triumphal procession and was welcomed into heaven with God's pronouncement from Matthew 25:21: "Well done, good and faithful servant!"

Loving Thoughts in Memory of Tim

Jerry Lewis, Chairman of Muscular Dystrophy Association: "Reading your letter and seeing the photo of Tim and me brought back some special memories. Thanks so much for your thoughtfulness in sharing these precious remembrances with me. Obviously, Tim's humanity and his generosity of spirit didn't arise out of a vacuum; it seems clear to me they were nurtured in a very loving and caring family environment. You should be proud of your accomplishment in helping Tim to be such an outstanding human being. . . . God bless you and your family."

Jim Quaid, volunteer for Association of Horizon and dear friend, remembered Tim in their newsletter (fall edition, November 1998): "Horizon has lost a true camp legend this past summer with the passing of Tim Stagg. For those of you who did not have the pleasure of meeting him, Tim was the kind of guy that could always brighten your day. He never had a bad thing to say, wore a smile from ear-to-ear, and had the greatest chuckle. It usually took Tim less than one hour upon arriving at the start of camp before he would have at least one "date" (a beautiful nurse no less) for our Friday night dinner/dance. At all of the dances, no one would start moving until Tim led the audience in "The Stagg"—a mind- and body-bending spectacle involving a cane being swung every which way. After an hour or so of pure energy, one of the nurses would try to convince Tim to take a breather for a few minutes. He would only concede if the nurse (usually more than one) would sit and chat with him. Tim was a charmer and a gentleman.

"We will miss the daily Cub updates, WGN news briefs, family stories, bad jokes, and the infamous bugle blowing to wake up the cabin. Most of all, we will miss his warm smile, his gentle personality, and his zest for life. Tim was an inspiration for many, and his memories will forever be a part of Camp Horizon.

"We are very grateful to Tim's family and friends for remembering Tim in their memorial donations to Horizon, which will be used to continue the summer camping experience that Tim loved so much."

John Driscoll, volunteer with Association of Horizon and friend: "I'm writing to tell you how sorry I was when I heard the news that Tim passed away. Tim was such a special guy, and he meant so much to all of us at Horizon. Back one year during the MDA camp, I was Tim's attendant and was close with him at each camp since then. While many will miss Tim's dancing exploits at camp, I'm going to miss just hanging out with him, hearing all about the extended Stagg family, taking boat rides with Tim with help from the health team, and building the annual 'stick house.' Tim's directness, honesty, and genuine concern for everyone else endeared him to me, and the entire Horizon camp. We're truly going to miss him."

Anne Gallagher, volunteer nurse, Association of Horizon, and friend: "I've known Tim from 'camp' for the last thirteen years, and it was always a heartwarming highlight to see him, talk with him, dance with him. Tim was an absolutely delightful person to be around, and he gave a lot of people a lot of joy. He suffered so much in the last years, and so I hope you find much comfort in the fact that he will not suffer any more. I know your life with him must have been full of many challenges, which it seems you handled with grace. He loved you so very much and always talked of his family and his nieces. Thank you for all the love and energy you gave to him and devoted to him. I hope that you feel rewarded for your efforts.

"One never knows what will happen in the course of a lifetime, but thankfully God's grace is abundant to those who ask for it and are willing to receive it. So I hope you feel His love and strength and joy surrounding you in times of hardship and grief. I'm so glad I knew Tim. He will be missed."

Melinda Campbell, social worker, Evanston Hospital: "I just learned of Tim's death today. I want you to know how many lives he and you have touched at Evanston Hospital—and in such a very positive, inspirational way. Thank you for letting God's love shine through your family."

NOTE: Someone from the hospital called and talked to Pat. They conveyed their sympathy and also let us know what the response was when the news about Tim's death circulated. They said that in spite of their training and experience with death every day, everyone, especially those in the intensive care unit, were so saddened, they openly—tearfully—showed their sorrow.

Sue (Schaefer) Low, teacher and friend: "Tim was one of my favorite students in my twenty-six years of teaching Special Ed. Each year he was one of the people I most looked forward to seeing at the Homecoming dance. Tim was an amazing person. His positive disposition and his delightful personality made him such a pleasure to teach and also to have as a friend. When I was his teacher we would always have a bet each year about who would have a better record—the Cubs or the White Sox. When school resumed in the fall, whoever has the worst record had to buy the winner a can of pop. He used to tease me at the dance each year about how many cans of pop I had to buy him back then.

"The dance wasn't the same for me this year, but as I saw old friends and former classmates of Tim's and we talked about how much we will miss him, Norman Glowacki said, 'Well, Mrs. Schaefer, I think he's here with us now anyway, even though we don't see him.' I think Norman was right. Tim will always hold a very special place in my heart and in my memories. You were wonderful parents to him and you raised him to be a fine young man. I'm sure he has a very special place in heaven."

Christmas 2000: "I continue to keep your family in my prayers. I have my 'Tim angel' on my tree again this year as a beautiful memory of your son."

Frank Prokop, Tim's godfather, wrote poetically: "As we look up to the sky and we ask the reason why, His life was one of much pain, but this great guy lived not in vain. He is where we want to be, in God's arms for eternity."

Mark Stewart, brother-in-law and friend, memorialized this way: "Our Tim—A son, a nephew, a cousin, an uncle, a friend and a brother, there never will be quite another. Always encouraging never putting down, of your favorite people there was Bozo the Clown. In all the years I've known you, you never complained of what life has dealt you, of the sorrow and pain. I've watched you for years through struggles and shame and then life's unfairness that you overcame. Many a strong man could not endure what you did, I'd cry out to our Lord, 'But he's only a kid.' A more faithful sports fan you'll never find—even if Chicago was way behind. Your personality is one we all love, you've been a gift sent from heaven above. Sports events a big part of you life—probably bigger than with most men's wives. But no matter how awful to others this present time seems. You know and I know you're finally in God's Field of Dreams."

Neighbor, Irv Jordahl, wrote this letter of encouragement: (Note: Irv had a stroke and is confined to his home. Kay and Tim would visit him and entertain him with music from Kay's guitar and Tim's tambourine.)

"I am proud to have a friend like Tim who always finds time to laugh and grin. With the rhythm within him he can make the tambourine sing. He plays for the rich and poor and by the dark and light of the moon. With his friend Kay they would play night or day to bring laughter and happiness to us all. One day my friend took a fall and hit his head on the wall. We thought it was over and Tim would no longer bring laughter and joy to us all. So we all prayed to the Lord and He answered our prayers one and all. He is now better and came home to his mother. With his friend Kay they will once again play and bring laughter and cheer to us all. From Mr. Jordahl across the street, we thank the Lord."

Summary of Information Mental Retardation Differences

God uses all situations to teach us and bring us to where He wants to use us for His glory.

Job 22:21: "Agree with God and be at peace; thereby good will come to you."

During the presidency of John F. Kennedy, issues of the mentally retarded were becoming more public. His sister was also mentally disabled and lived in a home for the handicapped in southern Wisconsin not too far from where we live. About one out of every ten Americans has a family member who is mentally retarded, about three out of every hundred. Its effects touch every social and economic background and nationality.

Mental retardation is a condition that does not allow the brain to develop to its full potential. It is not a disease and therefore should never be placed on the same par as mental illness. There is a vast difference between the two. The levels run the gamut from mild and moderate to severe and profound, and no two individuals are affected the same way. They are special, unique, beautiful people. The child who is labeled mentally retarded will live, interact, and function day-to-day in a world totally different than that of you and me.

Many causes of mental retardation are unknown or not fully understood, along with the more than 250 causes that are identifiable. Many different elements can be the cause of poor brain development before, during, or after childbirth. Certain situations or illness in early infancy can also be factors.

Autism is a disability with abnormal compulsive behaviors. It is a blend of significant disturbances in intellectual, sensory, cognitive, social, physiological, and emotional functioning. These children have difficulty with impaired language and communication, and abnormal social interaction. Parents with an autistic child deal with the ultimate in the area of frustration.

Cerebral palsy is caused by brain damage resulting from an injury before, during, or directly after birth. There is no cure, but the child can be helped with therapy and training. Palsy is described as an impairment or loss of sensation or the ability to control movement. Paralysis may also occur. It is not a progressive condition and mental retardation in some cases may not be a factor. However, estimates determine that almost 75 percent are mentally retarded as well.

Down syndrome is caused by a genetic irregularity and is the single most common cause of mental retardation. Some characteristic physical features may not be recognized immediately at birth. The Downs child has an extra chromosome coming from one or both of the parents. Three explanations are given for three different situations regarding the division of cells with the extra chromosome. One occurs before conception, during the formation of egg and sperm. One is after conception affecting the division of the growing, multiplying cells. And the third is when the chromosome attaches itself to another.

The above reasons listed for mental retardation are given in capsule form. The full story would take volumes to write. Tim's malfunction and retardation, according to the neurologist who put him on the prednisone, felt it was caused by the congenital polyneuritis. This happened during the developmental period before he was born.

Polyneuritis means involvement of many nerves and is sometimes confused with polio. No one knows what causes it. The disease affects the nerves just after they leave the spinal cord. Swelling and degeneration of the nerve occurs, and the muscles to the nerve supply become weak or paralyzed. The legs are most often affected, but the process may spread up the spinal column, picking up nerves to the rest of the body and affecting the arms. In some cases it is believed to be the result of a defective autoimmune mechanism. Scientists think it could result from an allergic reaction where an infection was the culprit. Most people overcome polyneuritis. Tim's was different. Along with this, many other problems like Charcot Marie Tooth were added to his record.

A Parent's Handbook

In 1979, *A Parent's Handbook, The World of the Developmentally Disabled Child* was published. Nothing was overlooked in this large informational manual. It covered every aspect of need for the handicapped, for parents and caregivers, and for those in the teaching and medical professions. It also provided information on the protective rights of the disabled and the Bill of Rights Act of 1975 that was legislated. The handicapped have the right to choose, to be able to agree or disagree. Legally, they have the right to their opinion when it involves their future and where they will live.

It was during this same time that changes were being made with the decline of institutionalization. More growth in mainstreaming or normalization was taking place. Federal and state funding and the rise of civil rights advocacy helped make special facilities and programs more available.

After 30 years of research, attitudes were beginning to change. The belief had been that those with mental disabilities were that way because of hereditary, and that they were unchangeable and socially harmful. Because of this belief, institutions existed so the handicapped would be separated from the "normal" population. This thinking began to change in 1925, but progress to get things moving in a positive direction didn't take root until the early 1950s.

It was with the efforts of parents to secure basic rights for their handicapped children that normalization and mainstreaming began. They demanded a proper education and training in a stimulating environment that would allow more freedom. This approach then became a national objective. During the 1970s and 1980s, community-based facilities were becoming popular, with the emphasis on community outreach, individualized training, and education. It expanded the treatment with ongoing care from birth through adulthood.

A Bureau of Education for the disabled was created in 1967, and in 1975 a law was passed ensuring an education for all handicapped children. At that time an estimated 8 million handicapped children were not receiving an adequate education, with 1 million being excluded entirely from the public school system. In 1963 the Vocational Education Act was passed, providing programs for vocational training.

I'm sure President Kennedy's concern for his sister inspired him to move toward a positive solution to the needs in this country. He was instrumental in proposing a national program to combat mental retardation with a range of services to meet the lifetime needs of those who are disabled.

This proved to be a major step in linking the federal government and local agencies in providing the handicapped with necessary provisions to live a more normal life. Both laws and customs of our land have denied the handicapped the rights enjoyed by other citizens.

During the 1980s, institutions in the United States became nothing more than warehouses for what they referred to as the "feebleminded." They went from facilities that were designed to be more like boarding schools where students who could be taught were placed. But in 1980, the custodial nature of caring became the norm for institutions. Once a person was committed to one of these facilities, it would be almost impossible for them to return to their homes or communities.

The numbers of children and adults housed in these institutions grew to such an extent that the facilities were overcrowded and understaffed, and the majority of those on staff had little or no training. Conditions were dehumanizing. Today, crowding is no longer a problem and most institutions are accredited just as hospitals are.

The main thrust is to have the handicapped live at home with their families, or in community-based homes. Jobs in the community are available to the handicapped today, with most of the training having come from special education programs through our public schools.

Being mentally retarded means the brain is not able to develop to its full potential. It is neither a mental disease nor mental illness. The two are totally different. Learning disabilities vary from extremely low to those who are close to normal, and no two individuals are affected in the same way. Each child is unique. Each child is very, very special. Thank you, Lord, for creating us in *Your* image and likeness.

To order additional copies of

SUNSHINE *on* *My* SHOULDER

Have your credit card ready and call:

1-877-421-READ (7323)

or please visit our web site at
www.pleasantword.com

Also available at: www.amazon.com

Printed in the United States
1308600001B/301-351

9 781579 216658